T0219836

Beginning Go Programming

Build Reliable and Efficient Applications with Go

Rumeel Hussain
Maryam Zulfiqar

Apress®

Beginning Go Programming: Build Reliable and Efficient Applications with Go

Rumeel Hussain
Dubai, United Arab Emirates

Maryam Zulfiqar
Lahore, Pakistan

ISBN-13 (pbk): 978-1-4842-8857-3
https://doi.org/10.1007/978-1-4842-8858-0

ISBN-13 (electronic): 978-1-4842-8858-0

Managing Director, Apress Media LLC: Welmoed Spahr
Acquisitions Editor: Celestin Suresh John
Development Editor: James Markham
Coordinating Editor: Mark Powers
Copy Editor: Kezia Endsley

Cover designed by eStudioCalamar

Cover image by Benjamin Davies on Unsplash (www.unsplash.com)

Distributed to the book trade worldwide by Apress Media, LLC, 1 New York Plaza, New York, NY 10004, U.S.A. Phone 1-800-SPRINGER, fax (201) 348-4505, e-mail orders-ny@springer-sbm.com, or visit www.springeronline.com. Apress Media, LLC is a California LLC and the sole member (owner) is Springer Science + Business Media Finance Inc (SSBM Finance Inc). SSBM Finance Inc is a **Delaware** corporation.

For information on translations, please e-mail booktranslations@springernature.com; for reprint, paperback, or audio rights, please e-mail bookpermissions@springernature.com.

Apress titles may be purchased in bulk for academic, corporate, or promotional use. eBook versions and licenses are also available for most titles. For more information, reference our Print and eBook Bulk Sales web page at http://www.apress.com/bulk-sales.

Any source code or other supplementary material referenced by the author in this book is available to readers on GitHub (https://github.com/Apress). For more detailed information, please visit http://www.apress.com/source-code.

Printed on acid-free paper

This book is dedicated to Rumeel's late mother and Abdullah Hassan.

Table of Contents

About the Authors

 **Rumeel Hussain** has a bachelor's degree in computer science and is presently working as a Blockchain Solution Architect at BNB Chain, supporting the development and growth of the BNB Chain ecosystem. He is an information technology enthusiast with more than five years of experience leading and implementing blockchain applications and architectures, analyzing and refactoring modern programming languages like Go, troubleshooting cloud infrastructure, and assessing security risks. His current work is focused on leveraging blockchain technology and crypto to achieve the full potential of Web3 applications.

Maryam Zulfiqar has four years of research experience and has a master's degree in computer science. She is currently working as a Tech Martian at BNB Chain. She also works as a senior researcher and developer. She is passionate about developer education, especially about sharing her knowledge on topics that are "the talk of the town" in the technology field. She has also worked in researcher and teamlead roles for HEC-funded projects targeted at community growth and welfare.

About the Technical Reviewer

Fabio Claudio Ferracchiati is a senior consultant and a senior analyst/
developer using Microsoft technologies. He works for BluArancio
(`www.bluarancio.com`). He is a Microsoft Certified Solution Developer for
.NET, a Microsoft Certified Application Developer for .NET, a Microsoft
Certified Professional, and a prolific author and technical reviewer.
Over the past ten years, he's written articles for Italian and international
magazines and coauthored more than ten books on a variety of
computer topics.

Preface

Google designed the Go language to be comprehensive yet be powerful enough to tackle big problems. It is a multi-paradigm programming language with built-in features for concurrent programming. It enables developers to easily build software that is simple, reliable, and efficient. This book is designed to provide knowledge to beginners and help them start developing great Go-based applications.

In this book, we cover the basics of the Go programming language and provide you with hands-on working experience through clear examples and recipes. From basic syntax formulation to providing insights into using the Go language to build concurrent programs and applications like HTTP servers and communication with REST APIs, this book covers it all.

This is a practical hands-on guide through which you will learn how to write Go code using clear examples that demonstrate the language in action. You'll also learn tips and tricks about the Go programming language for an efficient use.

CHAPTER 1

Introduction

Developed by Google in 2007, Go (aka GoLang) is a programming language designed with simplicity and speed as its focus. The design goals of Go were to create a simple and readable syntax of a dynamically-typed, high-level language programming language like Python, but also have the stability and efficiency of a statically-typed low-level language like C/C++. Supported by Google, Go is an open-source programming language and is easier to learn and get started with. It has built-in support for concurrency, a robust standard library, type safety, multiple built-in types, dynamic-typing capability, garbage collection, and several other advanced features, such as key-value maps and variable-length arrays. Go has the power to let you leverage the might that multi-core processors have to offer, which results in faster-running programs.

Is GoLang Static-Typed or Compiled?

Any programmer's natural concern about a programming language is whether the language is compiled or interpreted. JavaScript is an example of an interpreted language. Web browsers can directly read JavaScript source code and execute it at runtime. There is no pre-computation involved. Even though some interpreted environments can produce intermediate formats such as bytecode, there is no pre-computation step involved.

© Rumeel Hussain and Maryam Zulfiqar 2022
R. Hussain and M. Zulfiqar, *Beginning Go Programming*,
https://doi.org/10.1007/978-1-4842-8858-0_1

Compiled Programming Language

In contrast to an interpreted language, the source code of a compiled language is transformed into an operating system-specific format. Like C and C++, Go is a compiled language. However, compared to Java, whose source code is compiled into a format capable of running on different operating systems, Go's source code is compiled into an operating system-specific format. That means the code is executable only on the operating system for which it was compiled.

Statically-Typed Language

Go is a statically-typed language. That means its variables must have specific types. Nevertheless, it is not always mandatory to declare variables explicitly. The compiler can infer the types; however, at compilation time, the types are always known.

The capability to run a source code file without recompiling it can sometimes lead programmers to think that Go is an interpreted language. The real magic is in the background, where the source code is compiled into a temporary executable form. The compilation tool, "Go," is required to build applications delivered to users. This is because the compiled executable is in a format that is operating-system-specific. Each Go application consists of a statically-linked runtime. During the compilation process of the application, a runtime component is packaged with the executable format. This is why the size of applications built using the Go language is comparatively larger than the source code. No external virtual machine is involved, so it is necessary to include a runtime package.

Is Go an Object-Oriented Programming Language?

Go is not an object-oriented programming language. Nevertheless, you will find certain important object-oriented features in the Go language.

- Custom interfaces can be defined. In Go, an interface can be thought of as a contract that lays out a set of functions that must be implemented by any program that implements this interface.

- Custom types can be defined. Custom types can also have their own methods (functions). It's worth noting that in Go, practically everything is a type, and each type implements at least one interface.

- Custom structs (data structures) can be defined, containing member fields and methods.

Features that Make GoLang the Premium Choice for Programming

Other features of Go that make it popular among leading companies include the following:

- Go supports environment-adopting patterns identical to those offered by dynamic languages. For example, it supports type inference. That means that `intVariable:= 123` is a valid way to declare a type `int` variable named `intVariable` with a value of `123`.

- Go offers much faster compilation times.

- Go supports concurrency. For example, it offers the `select` statement, *goroutines,* which are similar to lightweight processes, and channels.

- Go programs are much simpler, more concise, and comparatively safer.

- Go supports type embedding and interfaces.

- Without the need for external dependencies, Go supports the production of statically-linked native binaries.

Intentionally Excluded Features from GoLang

In order to keep Go simple and concise, some of the features that are usually supported by similar programming languages are excluded from the Go language. The major reason for the omission is that Go's creators believed that all these factors make programming languages increasingly hard to comprehend and bug-prone. Some of the features that are excluded intentionally are as follows:

- Type inheritance (no classes)

- Generic programming

- Method or operator overloading

- Pointer arithmetic

- Structured exception handling

- Implicit numeric conversions

- Assertions

- Circular dependencies among packages

Go Programs

A Go program can be a minimum of three lines and extend to up to millions of lines. Go programs are written into text files having the `.go` extension, such as `myProgram.go`. Any text editor (like vim, vi, sublime, vs code, etc.) of your choice can be used to write Go programs. For efficient management of dependencies, Go programs are constructed using packages. The traditional compile and link model is used by the Go programming implementation to generate executable binaries.

Summary

The Go programming language was developed by Google in 2007. It was designed as a compiled language with simplicity and speed as its focus. The design goals of Go were to create a simple and readable syntax of a dynamically-typed high-level language programming language but also have the stability and efficiency of a statically-typed low-level language. It is an open-source programming language and is relatively easier to learn and get started with. Go comes with built-in support for concurrency, a robust standard library, type safety, multiple built-in types, dynamic-typing capability, garbage collection, and several other advanced features, including key-value maps and variable-length arrays.

Furthermore, Go has the power to let you leverage the might that multi-core processors have to offer, which results in faster-running programs. One of the important aspects to remember about Go is that it is not an object-oriented programming language. Nevertheless, you do find certain important object-oriented features in the Go language, like custom interfaces, types, and structs (data structures), which can be defined.

Certain features have been excluded from Go to meet its design goals. The major reason for these omissions is that Go's creators believed that all these factors make programming languages increasingly hard to comprehend and bug-prone.

The next chapter takes a dive deep into the programming fundamentals of Go, along with practical recipes that provide hands-on examples of the concepts.

CHAPTER 2

Go Basics

What makes Go an easy-to-learn language is that everything you need to know about a Go program is right on the surface. There is no need to remember any language rules, as they are all in the application code. This chapter covers the basics of the Go programming language, like accepting input, using math operators and packages, managing memory, using different data structures, and understanding the program flow of a Go-based application. It also covers using functions and returning multiple values, as well as reading and writing data to files and handling JSON data.

Ancestors of Go

Go is based on a number of different languages. It was originally designed to be the next generation of the C language. It's capable of performing everything you can do with C, including system programming, application development, and so on.

Go Syntax

Go borrows a lot of its syntax from C and its related languages—C++, C#, Java, and so on. Along with this, it also borrows syntax from Pascal, Modula, Oberon, and other similar languages. One of the biggest attractions of Go is that its programs are very concise because of the precise and

© Rumeel Hussain and Maryam Zulfiqar 2022
R. Hussain and M. Zulfiqar, *Beginning Go Programming*,
https://doi.org/10.1007/978-1-4842-8858-0_2

comprehensive set of keywords and syntax. In order to be effective with any language, you have to know the certain basic syntax rules of that particular language. The following is a list of some of the most important syntax rules set by the designers of the Go programming language.

1. **Case sensitivity**

   - You must spell *identifiers* like functions, variables, and type names in the exact manner mentioned in the official documentation (`https://go.dev/doc/`).

   - Names for packages and variables use lowercase and mixed case.

   - Methods and fields of a type are initial capped.

   - In Go, initial uppercase characters indicate a special purpose.

     - Equivalent to the `public` keyword in other high-level programming languages like C++, C#, Java, and so on, in Go, an initial uppercase character indicates that the symbol is exported.

     - Similarly, equivalent to the `private` keyword, in Go, a lowercase initial character indicates that the particular method or variable is not exported nor accessible by the rest of the application other than the code block it is declared in.

2. **Semicolons can be skipped**

   - For the sake of reducing the amount of typing a developer has to do, as shown in Listing 2-1, Go eliminates semicolons from the ends of lines. This means that line feeds end the statement and no semicolons are required.

Listing 2-1. Semicolons Are Not Required as End-of-Line Indicators

```
var color [2] string
colors[0] = "black"
colors[1] = "white"
```

Even though the language specification requires semicolons, it is not necessary to type them explicitly. Thanks to Lexer, the software component that parses the code and analyses it, semicolons are added during the compilation process as needed.

The Rule Followed by Lexer for Adding Semicolons

When a statement is determined to be complete and Lexer encounters a line feed, meaning it's the end of the statement and the developer has not explicitly added a semicolon, Lexer will do so.

Note   You can't always add line feeds freely or break up statements with extra line feeds, as you can in other languages, because in certain cases they can be misinterpreted by Lexer.

3. **Code blocks with braces**

- Code blocks, i.e., multiple lines of code that are intended to be grouped together, are wrapped within braces. See Listing 2-2.

Listing 2-2. Braces Are Used to Indicate Code Blocks

```
sum := 0
for i :=0; i<10; i++{
  sum += i
}
fmt.Println(sum) //prints '45'
```

In Listing 2-2, the variable named sum is declared
and then assigned a value of zero. The for loop is
initialized from 0 to 10 and is used to increment the
value of the sum by i. After the loop terminates, the
value stored in the sum variable is printed using a
function called Println or "print line". Println is a
built-in function of the package called FMT. The code
that you want to iterate over is wrapped between
two braces. Note that it is important to make sure
that the opening brace is on the same line as any
preceding statement.

4. **Built-in functions**

- Go supports a set of several built-in functions that
  are always available in your code without having to
  import anything. These functions are members of a
  special package named Builtin. The Go compiler
  assumes that the Builtin package is always
  imported. Example functions include the following:

  - len(string) returns the length of the string.

  - panic(error) stops execution and displays an
    error message.

  - recover() manages the behavior of a panicking
    goroutine.

For more information, you can visit the official
documentation of the builtin package at
https://pkg.go.dev/builtin.

Installing Go

To install the Go compiler, visit https://go.dev/dl/ and download the binary release suitable for your system. Just run the installer to install the compiler on your system.

In order to verify your installation, on Windows OS, open the command prompt and type go version, as illustrated in Figure 2-1. The output shows the version of the Go compiler installed on your system.

```
$ go version
go version go1.17.6 windows/amd64
```

Figure 2-1. *Output showing the installed version of Go*

If you type the path command at the command prompt, you can see where all the Go executable commands are saved. If you can see the path to the directory where Go is installed, e.g. C:\Users\UserName\go\bin, you are ready to build programs in Go.

To find the directory where Go is installed on macOS, open a terminal window and type export $PATH. Upon successful execution, a listing of the directory, indicating the path to the bin folder where Go was installed, e.g., user/local/go/bin, is shown. In addition, along with the addition of the command to execute Go programs to the directory phrase, a file is added to a path under the root. To ensure that you can run Go programs from anywhere, go to your home directory and type go version. If everything's working correctly, you should see output indicating the version of the Go language that you're using, as shown in Figure 2-2.

```
● ● ●                    ⚡ instructor — -bash — 80×24
Last login: Wed Jan 20 14:29:23 on ttys000
NAMER-R-M08:~ instructor$ export $PATH
-bash: export: `/usr/local/bin:/usr/bin:/bin:/usr/sbin:/sbin:/usr/local/go/bin:/
Users/instructor/Library/Android/sdk/platform-tools': not a valid identifier
NAMER-R-M08:~ instructor$ cd /etc/paths.d
NAMER-R-M08:paths.d instructor$ ls
go
NAMER-R-M08:paths.d instructor$ nano go
NAMER-R-M08:paths.d instructor$ cd /
NAMER-R-M08:/ instructor$ cd ~
NAMER-R-M08:~ instructor$ go version
go version go1.15.7 darwin/amd64
NAMER-R-M08:~ instructor$ █
```

Figure 2-2. *Checking the PATH variable and version to ensure correct installation of Go Compiler*

If you can see the version, you're ready to start programming using the Go language. The first element you'll want to explore is the Go Playground.

Go Playground

One of the fastest ways to start coding and developing Go-based programs is by using the Go Playground (`https://go.dev/play/`), a web-based IDE. As shown in Figure 2-3, without having to install anything, Go Playground allows users to edit, run, and experiment with the Go programming language. When the Run button is clicked, the Go Playground compiles and executes the Go code on Google servers and outputs the result of the execution.

Figure 2-3. *The Go Playground IDE*

The Go Playground is a completely free-to-use service with no limitations. There are no requirements for user registration or licensing fees. Furthermore, it has no limitations on the number of source code files you can work with or the number of times you can run your code. It is a great way to test your Go code without creating or compiling any local source files. Nonetheless, there are other several IDEs available that can be used to develop Go applications.

Developing Go Applications Using IDEs

There isn't a single integrated development environment (IDE) for good programming that's endorsed or even developed by the Go development team. There are, however, many plug-ins for commercial and open-source IDEs that have been created by the Go community or by IDE vendors, which you choose mostly depending on what development environments you're already familiar with. In this book, we use Go Playground and Visual Studio Code to write and run Go programs. Let's jump into how to get started programming Go applications.

13

Getting Started Programming Go Applications

Once you've installed the Go development tools, you are ready to create as many Go applications as you like. Usually, a Go program is constructed of the following parts:

- Declaring package name

- Importing package(s)

- Declaring and defining function(s)

- Variable(s)

- Expressions and statements

- Comment(s)

Let's Print Hello World!

Prior to learning about the Go programming language's basic building blocks, knowing about the bare minimum structure of Go programs is important. Listing 2-3 illustrates how to print the "Hello World!" message on the screen as output. Even though the program is concise and has minimum functionality, it is adequate for understanding Go's program structure.

Listing 2-3. Basic Program that Illustrates Different Parts of a Go Program

```
package main

import (
    "fmt"
)
```

```
// Singe-Line Comment
/*
    Multi
    Line
    Comment
*/
func main(){
        fmt.Println("Hello, World ! ")
}
```

Different parts of a Go program

Listing 2-3 explains the different parts of the following Go program:

- **Packages:** In the first line of a Go program, packages are always mentioned. In Listing 2-3, the statement package main indicates the name of the package to which the program belongs. This statement is mandatory because, in Go, all programs are organized and run in packages. For any program, the starting point of execution is the main package. Furthermore, with every package, a path and name are associated.

- **Import:** The import keyword is used to import different packages the application will use. It is a preprocessor directive that instructs the Go compiler to include all the files in the mentioned package. In the previous example, we imported the fmt (format) package, which provides different functions for formatting input and output.

- **Comments:** In Go, double forward-slashes // are used to indicate a single-line comment in code. Multi-line comments are enclosed with the /* */ block.

- **Func:** The func keyword is used to declare functions; in this case, a function named main. It is important to enclose the body of each function within curly braces {}. This is necessary for the Go compiler to know where each function starts and ends.

- **Main function:** Execution starts at the main function in the main package, which makes the main identifier very important. The compiler will throw an error if the main function is excluded.

- One of the built-in functions available in the fmt package is the Println(...) function. By importing the fmt package, you also export the Println method. The Println function is used to display output on the screen.

- In Go, identifiers that are capitalized indicate that the particular identifier is exported, for example, the initial letter of the Println method is a capital letter. In Go, the term "exported" means the function, constant, or variable can be accessed by the importer of that particular package.

How to Execute a Go Program

In order to execute the program, click the Run button on the Go Playground. Your code will be compiled and executed on Google servers and the output will be displayed on the screen.

To execute your program using the command prompt on Windows, you can use the go run filename.go command. For example, as in shown in Figure 2-4, the command used to run Listing 2-3 is go run main.go. To build applications, run the go build filename.go command. For example, to build the sample program, you'd issue the command go build main.go. To run the compiled version of the program, you'd issue the ./filename command, for example, ./main.

16

```
> go run main.go
Hello, World !
> go build main.go
> ./main
Hello, World !
```

Figure 2-4. *Commands to run and build a Go program*

Interestingly, the compiled application runs faster than the go run command. Building the source code file will result in the creation of a compiled binary file specifically designed to work on your current operating system. Even though it is possible to compile your programs for other operating systems, by default, the compiler will generate the binary compatible with your operating system.

Keywords

Like every programming language, Go has a set of keywords (words reserved for special purposes). These keywords cannot be used as identifier names for contents, variables, functions, or any other purpose. Table 2-1 includes a list of Go's keywords.

Table 2-1. *Go's Keywords*

chan	const	goto	interface	struct
defer	case	func	var	select
break	for	go	import	continue
default	fallthrough	switch	type	range
if	else	return	package	map

Now that you are aware of its keywords, you are ready to learn how to use variables and other data structures in Go.

Variables

Like other programming languages, variables are used in Go to store data in memory. Being a statically-typed language, Go requires that each variable be assigned a type. Once a type is assigned it cannot be changed. There are two ways to set the type for a variable—explicitly or implicitly. By explicitly, we mean that at the time of declaration, the name of the type is mentioned. Implicitly means that, based on the variable's initial value, the compiler will infer the type.

In Go, every variable should have a type. The type plays an important role in determining the layout and size of the variable's memory, the allowed value ranges, and the set of operations applicable to the variable.

Variable Data Types

Go allows user-defined types and comes with various built-in data types. Here are a few basic built-in data types available in Go:

- **Boolean:** Bool represents Boolean data in the form of true/false. True and false are the only two values that a Boolean data type can be assigned.

- **String:** In Go, a variable of string type contains a series of characters.

- Numeric data types:

    - **Integers:** Used to store whole numbers.

        - **Fixed Integer:** Included formats are uint8, uint16, uint32, int8, int16, and int 32. These are used to declare unsigned or signed integers. The numbers in the name of the formats are the bits that have an effect on the range of numbers that a variable can be assigned.

- **Float:** Used to store floating-point numbers. Supported formats include float32 and float64.

- **Complex:** Complex numbers contain two parts: the real number and imaginary number. Supported formats are complex64 and complex128.

- **Aliases:** These can be used instead of full type names, such as byte (same as uint8), uint (32 or 64 bits), rune (same as int32), int (same as uint), and uintptr (an unsigned integer that is used to store uninterpreted bits of a pointer value).

- **Data collections:** Go also has built-in types for different data collections.

  - **Arrays and slices:** Used to manage ordered data collections.

  - **Maps and structs:** Used to manage aggregations of values.

  - **Enumeration:** Used to store a set of named constant values.

- Language organization types:

  - **Function:** Go considers function a type. This allows the passing of one function as an argument to another.

  - **Interfaces:** Used to specify a set of one or more method signatures.

  - **Channels:** Used to connect goroutines.

- Data management:

  - **Pointers:** Store direct addresses of memory locations (variables).

Other than the built-in types, Go also allows programmers to create user-defined data types.

Variable Naming Conventions

A variable name can be made up of letters, digits, and underscores. However, the variable name should begin with either an underscore or a letter. The lower- and uppercase letters are treated differently, because of the case-sensitive nature of the Go language.

Declaring Variables

As Go is statically-typed, it requires you to set the type (explicitly or implicitly) of each variable used in your program during the compilation process. The assigned type cannot be changed at runtime.

Listing 2-4 illustrates the different ways of declaring and assigning a type to variables in Go. In the explicit declaration of a variable, the var keyword is used, after which the name and type of the variable are mentioned. For example, as shown in lines # 8 and 12, assigning an initial value is optional. Line#10 uses placeholders in the print function to print the values stored in the variables along with a message. Note that Printf doesn't add the line feed automatically and hence we added the \n for a line feed.

Listing 2-4. Ways to Declare Variables in Go

```go
package main

import(
        "fmt"
)

func main() {{
        //Explicit Declaration
        var aStringVariable string = "i am a string"
        fmt.Println(aStringVariable)
        fmt.Printf("Printing variable along text: %s \n",
        aStringVariable)

        var anotherStringVariable string
        fmt.Println(anotherStringVariable)
        fmt.Printf("Printing variable along text: %s \n",
        anotherStringVariable)

        var defaultInt int
        fmt.Println(defaultInt)

        //Implicit Declaration
        myString := "Implicit Declaration of string"
        fmt.Println(myString)
}
```

In the case of implicit declaration, the variable type is inferred based on the initial value assigned to the variable. Line#20 in Listing 2-4 illustrates implicit declaration. Note that the := operator only works for variable declarations inside of functions. The var keyword has to be used to declare variables outside the functions.

The var statement can also be used to declare a list of variables, as shown in Figure 2-5.

```
var (                           var (
      name    string                  name, location  string
      age     int                     age             int = 45
      location string                 phone int
)                               )
var (
      name, location, age = "Prince Oberyn", "Dorne", 32
)
```

Figure 2-5. *Different ways of declaring variables in Go*

To declare constants, programmers must use the const keyword.
Figure 2-6 illustrates how constants can be declared in a Go program.

```
const aConstantVariable int = 64

const AnotherConstantVariable int = 64
```

Figure 2-6. *Declaring constants in Go*

Constants are always declared outside of functions. If the name of the
constant variable starts with a lowercase letter, that means it's available for
use only by the functions of the program (like the private keyword). The
variable is public when its name begins with a capital letter.

Taking User Input

In the previous section, you learned about the use of the fmt package
through which you can output different messages on the screen. This
section demonstrates how to read user input from the console, store it in
variables, or echo it to the screen. Note that standard input (stdin) is a
stream that is used to read input data.

One important point to remember regarding Go Playground is that it
does not support interactive programs and hence cannot read from os.
Stdin. Due to this, it is better to use other IDEs, like Visual Studio or Code,
to test the code in this book whenever user input is required.

In Go, the OS and IO packages contain different functions for reading the standard input from the console. These sets of functions are used to scan formatted text and extract values.

- Scan, Scanf, and Scanln can be used to read input from os.Stdin.

- Fscan, Fscanf, and Fscanln can be used to read input from a specified io.Reader.

- Sscan, Sscanf, and Sscanln can be used to read input from an argument string.

Using scanf

In order to use the Scanf function, you must import the fmt package. It is used to specify which way the input should be read. The Scanf function scans the text input from stdin and stores the space-separated values into consecutive arguments as defined in the string format. The count of successfully scanned items is also returned by the Scanf function. If the returned number of items is less than the specified arguments, the function will throw an error. This is because it is mandatory for newline feeds in the input to match the newlines specified in the format. Listing 2-5 illustrates the use of the Scanf function for taking user input.

Listing 2-5. Using the Built-In Scanf Function to Take User Input

```
package main

import (
        "fmt"
)

func main() {
        var name string
        var age int
```

```
        fmt.Print("Enter Your name: ")
        fmt.Scanf("%s", &name)
        fmt.Println("Hello ", name)

        fmt.Print("Enter Your age: ")
        fmt.Scan(&age)
        fmt.Println("Your age is ", age)
}
```

Output:

```
Enter your name: Maryam
Hello Maryam
Enter your age: 30
Your age is 30
```

Using ScanIn

Scanln scans the text from stdin; however, it stops scanning when a newline is encountered. Therefore, it is necessary to place a newline character or EOF after the final item to indicate the end of input. Listing 2-6 illustrates the use of Scanln.

Listing 2-6. Using the Scanln Built-In Function to Take User Input in Go

```
package main

import (
        "fmt"
)

func main() {
        var name string
        var age int
```

```go
        fmt.Print("Enter your name: ")
        fmt.Scanln(&name)
        fmt.Println("Hello ", name)

        fmt.Print("Enter your age: ")
        fmt.Scanln(&age)
        fmt.Println("Your age is ", age)

        var anInt int = 5
        var aFloat float64 = 42
        sum := float64(anInt) + aFloat
        fmt.Printf("Sum: %v, Type: %T \n", sum, sum)
}
```

/*Output:

```
Enter your name: Maryam
Hello Maryam
Enter your age: 30
Your age is 30*/
```

Scan vs Reader Functions

To split space-delimited tokens, you use the Scan functions and to read full lines, you used the reader function.

Using bufio

Buffered I/O is implemented via the bufio package. The bufio package wraps the io.Writer or io.Reader objects and returns a new Writer or Reader object, which has the necessary interface implemented for utility methods. This wrapping also provides textual I/O assistance and buffering.

In Listing 2-7, Line#11 declares two variables, one that stores the input. The second is an error object that stores any error messages.

Listing 2-7. Using the bufio Built-In Function to Take User Input in Go

```
1   package main
2   import(
3       "bufio"
4       "fmt"
5       "os"
6   )
7
8   func main(){
9           reader := bufio.NewReader(os.Stdin)
10          fmt.Print("Enter Some Text: ")
11          input, _ := reader.ReadString('\n')
12          fmt.Println("You have entered: ", input)
13  }
```

Output:

```
Enter Text: Hi! I am the author
You entered: Hi! I am the author
```

As illustrated, if you want to ignore a variable in Go, you name it with an underscore.

Now that you know how to use variables and take user input in your Go programs, it is time to learn how to use different math operators in Go.

Math Operators and Packages

Go supports the same set of mathematical operators as other C-style languages, including the usual arithmetic operators, all the bitwise operators, assignment operators, and relational operators. Tables 2-2 through 2-6 list all of the operators in Go.

Table 2-2. *List of Arithmetic Operators in Go*

Arithmetic	**+**	Sum operator is used for addition.
Operators	**-**	Difference operator is used for finding differences.
	*****	Multiply operator is used for finding products.
	/	Quotient operator is used for finding the quotient after division.
	%	Remainder operator is used for finding the remainder after division.
	--	Decrement operator decreases one from the value of its operand and stores the result in the operand.
	++	Increment operator increases one from the value of its operand and stores the result in the operand.

Table 2-3. *List of Bitwise Operators in Go*

Bitwise	**&**	Binary AND operator. If the bit is present in both operands, the binary and operator copy it to the result.
Operators	**|**	Binary OR operator. If the bit is present in either of the operands, the binary or operator copies it to the result.
	^	Bitwise XOR operator. If the bit is set in any operand, the bitwise xor operator copies the bit.
	&^	Bit clear.
	<<	Left shift operator. Shifts the left operand's value to the left by the number of bits specified by the right operand.
	>>	Right shift operator. Shifts the left operand's value to the right by the number of bits specified by the right operand.

Table 2-4. *List of Relational Operators in Go*

Relational Operators	==	Checks if the two operands have equal values, if they do, it returns true.
	!=	Checks if the two operands have unequal values, if they do, it returns true.
	>	Checks if the left operand is greater than the right operand, if it is, it returns true.
	<	Checks if the left operand is less than the right operand, if it is, it returns true.
	<=	Checks if the left operand is less than or equal to the right operand, if it is, it returns true.
	>=	Checks if the left operand is greater than or equal to the right operand, if it is, it returns true.

Table 2-5. *List of Logical Operators in Go*

Logical Operators	&&	Logical AND operator. Returns false is both operands are `false` and `true` if both the operands are true.
	||	Logical OR operator. Returns `true` if any of the operands are true.
	!	Logical NOT operator. Reverses the logical state of its operand, i.e., changes true to false and vice versa.

Table 2-6. *List of Assignment Operators in Go*

Assignment Operator	=	Simple assignment operator. The left operand is assigned the value of the right operand. For example, Z=X+Y will assign Z the calculated value of X+Y.
	+=	Add and assignment operator. The value stored in the right operand is added to the value of the left operand and the result is assigned to the left operand.
		For example, X += Y is equivalent to X = X + Y.
	-=	Subtract and assignment operator. The value stored in the right operand is subtracted from the value of the left operand and the result is assigned to the left operand.
		For example, X -= Y is equivalent to X = X − Y.
	*=	Multiply and assignment operator. The value stored in the right operand is multiplied by the value of the left operand and the result is assigned to the left operand.
		For example, X *= Y is equivalent to X = X * Y.
	/=	Divide and assignment operator. The value stored in the right operand is divided by the value of the left operand and the result is assigned to the left operand.
		For example, X /= Y is equivalent to X = X / Y.
	%=	Modulus and assignment operator. The value stored in the right operand is divided by the value of the left operand and the remainder of the division is assigned to the left operand.
		For example, X %= Y is equivalent to X = X % Y.
	<<=	Left shift and assignment operator. The value of the left operand is shifted to the left by the number of times specified by the right operand.
		For example, X <<= 1 is equivalent to X = X << 1.

(continued)

Table 2-6. (*continued*)

>>=	Right shift and assignment operator. The value of the left operand is shifted to the right by the number of times specified by the right operand.	
	For example, X >>= 1 is equivalent to X = X >> 1.	
&=	Bitwise AND assignment operator. For example, Y &= 3 is equivalent to Y=Y&3.	
^=	Bitwise exclusive OR and assignment operator. For example, Y ^= 3 is equivalent to Y = Y ^ 3	
|=	Bitwise inclusive OR and assignment operator. For example, Y |= 3 is equivalent to Y = Y | 2.	

Note that Go doesn't support implicit conversion of numeric types. This means that, for example, you cannot take an integer value and add it to a floating-point value without converting it.

Listing 2-8 contains two variables, one an integer and another a float. When you try to add them, this will result in the "invalid operation" error, crashing the application.

Listing 2-8. Illustration of Go Not Supporting Implicit Conversion of Numeric Types

```
var anInt int = 5
var aFloat float32 = 42
sum := anInt + aFloat  //invalid operation
fmt.Printf("Sum: %v, Type: %T \n", sum, sum)
```

Output:

⊗ invalid operation: mismatched types int and float64 compiler(MismatchedTypes) [Ln 19, Col 9]

In order to correctly perform this operation, you must convert one of these variables to match the type of the other. To achieve this goal, you have to wrap the value in the target type as a function call, as shown in Listing 2-9.

Listing 2-9. Explicit Conversion of Numeric Types in Go

```
var anInt int = 5
var aFloat float32 = 42
sum := float32(anInt) + aFloat
fmt.Printf("Sum: %v, Type: %T \n", sum, sum)
```

Output:

```
Sum: 47, Type: float32
```

The Math Package

To perform different math operations, you use the Math package. It contains different functions and constants like pi. Go offers many tools for mathematical operations, operators and members of the math package, including functions and constants. Listing 2-10 illustrates the use of functions and constants from the Math package. For more information on the Math package, refer to the official documentation at https://pkg. go.dev/math.

Listing 2-10. Basic Program Illustrating the Use of the Math
Package in Go

```go
package main

import (
        "fmt"
        "math"
)

func main() {
        i1, i2, i3 := 12, 45, 68
        intSum := i1 + i2 + i3
        fmt.Println("Integer Sum: ", intSum)

        f1, f2, f3 := 23.5, 65.1, 76.3
        floatSum := f1 + f2 + f3
        fmt.Println("Float Sum: ", floatSum)

        floatSum = math.Round(floatSum)
        fmt.Println("Rounded Sum is: ", floatSum)

        floatSum = math.Round(floatSum*100) / 100
        fmt.Println("Sum Rounded To Nearest 2 Decimals: ",
        floatSum)

        circleRadius := 15.6
        circumference := circleRadius * 2 * math.Pi
        fmt.Printf("Circumference: %.2f\n", circumference)
}
```

Dates and Times

In the Go language, the time package is used to manage the dates and times types. Declaring a variable with type as time encapsulates everything required for both times and dates type of data, which includes time zone management, math operations, and so on. Listing 2-11 illustrates the use of the time package.

Listing 2-11. Basic program Illustrating the Use of the Time Package in Go

```go
package main

import (
        "fmt"
        "time"
)

func main() {
        now := time.Now()
        fmt.Println("Current Time is: ", now)

        formatDate := time.Date(2009, time.November, 10, 23, 0,
        0, 0, time.UTC)
        fmt.Println("Go was launched at: ", formatDate)
        fmt.Println(formatDate.Format(time.ANSIC))

        parsedTime, _ := time.Parse(time.ANSIC, "Tue Nov 10
        23:00:00 2009")
        fmt.Printf("The type of parsedTime is %T\n", parsedTime)
}
```

Output:

```
Current Time is:   2022-08-29 21:06:14.02792 +0500 PKT
m=+0.003998301
Go was launched at:   2009-11-10 23:00:00 +0000 UTC
Tue Nov 10 23:00:00 2009
The type of parsedTime is time.Time
```

Listing 2-11 illustrates the use of the time package for using date and time types. In the example, in Line#10, a variable named now is declared. It will be initialized using the built-in time.Now() function, which returns a timestamp containing the current date, time, and time zone. It is also possible in Go for users to create their own explicit date and time values. Line#14 declares a variable named formatDate, which is initialized using the time.Date() function. The Date() function returns the time in the appropriate zone according to a given location corresponding to the format yyyy-mm-dd hh:mm:ss + nsec nanoseconds. You can also use a formatted version of the daytime value, as shown in Line#18. The Format() function returns a textual representation of the time value formatted as per the layout defined by the argument. This example uses the ANSIC format, but you can refer to the official documentation at https://pkg.go.dev/time#Time.Format for other standard formats.

In Listing 2-12, the Parse() function returns the time value representation of a string after parsing it.

Listing 2-12. Using the Parse Function from the Time Package

```
parsedTime, _ := time.Parse(time.ANSIC, "Tue Nov 10
23:00:00 2009")
fmt.Printf("The type of parsedTime is %T \n", parsedTime)
```

Output:

```
The type of parsedTime is time.Time
```

Since the Parse() function can return an error object, in this example, we added an underscore to ignore the object. The time object has many other useful functions. For example, you can add dates and perform special kinds of formatting, and so on. There are also patterns available that give you complete flexibility in how to format daytime values. The functions and constants in the time package give you all the tools you need to store and manage the date and time values. For more on this topic, refer to the official documentation on the time package at https://pkg.go.dev/time.

Operators Precedence in Go

Operator precedence refers to the criteria that determine the grouping of terms in an expression. It also affects the result of the expression evaluation. Like other programming languages, in Go, there is a pre-defined order of precedence of the operators, where some have higher precedence over the others. For example, the division operator / has higher precedence over the subtraction operator -.

Consider the statement a = 56 + 4 * 8 Here, variable a is assigned the value 88, not 480. This is because the multiply operator * has higher precedence over the addition operator +. Therefore, 4 * 8 is multiplied first and then the obtained result is added to 56.

Table 2-7 lists the operators from highest to lowest precedence. In a given expression, after scanning it from left to right, first, the operators having higher precedence are evaluated.

Table 2-7. *List of Operator Precedence in Go*

Category	Operator	Associativity
Postfix	**( ) [ ] -> . ++ - -**	Left to right
Unary	**+ - ! ~ ++ - - (type)* & sizeof**	Right to left
Multiplicative	*** / %**	Left to right
Additive	**+ -**	Left to right
Shift	**<< >>**	Left to right
Relational	**< <= > >=**	Left to right
Equality	**== !=**	Left to right
Bitwise AND	**&**	Left to right
Bitwise XOR	**^**	Left to right
Bitwise OR	**|**	Left to right
Logical AND	**&&**	Left to right
Logical OR	**||**	Left to right
Assignment	**= += -= *= /= %=>>= <<= &= ^= |=**	Right to left
Comma	**,**	Left to right

Memory Management and Reference Values

The Go runtime is required to run Go applications using the go run command on your system. The runtime is also included in the compiled and build binary Go application. Either way, like in any marked language, such as Java and C#, Go applications rely on the runtime that operates silently in the background utilizing dedicated threads for memory management. The advantage of the runtime is the elimination of the need to explicitly duplicate or allocate memory in the code.

New vs Make

It is critical to ensure that complex types, such as maps, are appropriately initialized. To initialize the complex objects in the Go programming language, there are two built-in functions—make and new. Be careful using them, as there is a difference between the two.

The new function only allocates memory for the complex object but does not initialize the memory. When an object, say a map, is allocated using the new function, it only returns the memory address of where that map is located. However, there is zero memory storage associated with the map object. Therefore, when a key-value pair is added to the map, it will throw an error.

Contrary to this, the make function allocates as well as initializes the memory for the map object created using the make function. It returns the memory address, like the new function, and the storage is initialized to non-zero. This means the map object can accept values without throwing errors.

Incorrect Memory Allocation Example

Listing 2-13 illustrates the incorrect memory allocation of map objects. A map object named string_map is declared on Line#1 using the new function. The map object accepts keys as strings and the associated values as integers. On Line#2, a key-value pair is added as an entry to the declared map object, where the key is named Marks and the associated value is 56.

Listing 2-13. Illustration of Incorrect Memory Allocation of Map Objects

```
string_Map := new(map[string]int)
string_Map["Marks"] = 56
fmt.Println(string_Map)
```

At runtime, Listing 2-13 will make the application crash and an error is thrown, as shown in Figure 2-7. This error is raised because you are attempting to place data in a map that does not have any memory storage initialized.

```
>go run mem-allocation-eg.go
# command-line-arguments
.\mem-allocation-eg.go:9:12: invalid operation: string_map["Marks"] (type *map[string]int does not support indexing)
```

Figure 2-7. *Error raised due to incorrect memory allocation of map object*

Correct Memory Allocation Example

The correct way to allocate memory for a complex object like the map is to warp your declaration in the make function, as shown in Listing 2-14. The make function will also initialize non-zero storage memory for the object.

Listing 2-14. Illustration of Correct Memory Allocation of Map Object

```go
string_Map := make(map[string]int)
string_Map["Marks"] = 56
fmt.Println(string_Map)
```

This time, when you initialize the object with the make function and try to add new entries to the map object, the code will successfully compile and run without errors, as shown in the output in Figure 2-8. Remember that when using complex objects, it is highly important to use the make function for initialization if you need to add data to the object immediately.

```
>go run mem-allocation-eg.go
map[Marks:56]
```

Figure 2-8. *Output after correct memory allocation*

Memory Deallocation

Memory deallocation is performed in an autonomous fashion by the *garbage collector* (GC) that comes packaged with the Go runtime. When the garbage collector is triggered while working in the background, it searches for objects that are either out of scope or set to nil, so it may clear away the memory and return it to your memory pool.

In Go version 1.5, the garbage collector was completely reconstructed to have very low latency for effectively reducing the number of pauses that occur while running Go applications. In the latest version, 1.18.3, the performance of the garbage collector while performing memory allocation is much faster and is also almost unnoticeable even on slower computers. For more information on garbage collectors, refer to the official documentation on runtime at `https://pkg.go.dev/runtime` and the talk release of the garbage collector improvement at `https://talks.golang.org/2015/go-gc.pdf`.

Pointers Data Type

Every variable is essentially a memory location. Note also that each memory location has a defined address as well. In Go, the ampersand (&) operator indicates a memory address and is used to access the address of a variable.

What Is a Pointer?

Pointers are in essence variables that have the capability of storing memory addresses of other variables. Note that a memory address refers to the direct address of the variable. A pointer can be declared with any data type, however, initializing it, i.e., storing the address of another variable, is not necessary. Similar to high-level languages, Go also supports pointers. Pointers are useful in Go to perform different tasks, for example, without the use of pointers you cannot perform a call by reference.

Declaring Pointers in Go

It is necessary to declare a pointer before its use, like any other variable or constant. The general syntax for declaring a pointer variable in Go is var variable_name *variable-type. Here, variable-type indicates the base type of the pointer. Make sure that the selected base type is a valid Go data type. variable-name indicates the pointer's name. One of the most important things that differentiates pointer declarations from other variable declarations is the asterisk (*) operator. In this statement, the asterisk indicates that the declared variable is a pointer. Listing 2-15 illustrates some valid examples of pointer declarations.

Listing 2-15. Different Ways of Declaring Pointers in Go

```
var intPointer   *int       /* pointer to an integer variable */
var floatPointer  *float32  /* pointer to a float variable */
var strPointer *string      /* pointer to a string variable */
```

It should be noted that, irrespective of its type, the inherent data type of value stored in all pointers is the same, i.e., a long hexadecimal number. This represents memory addresses, as all addresses are in the long hexadecimal format. The data type of the variable or constant that a pointer points to is the only differentiation between pointers of different data types. Furthermore, the value of the pointer can also be set to nil manually in the case of strings and automatically if the pointer is not initialized at the time of declaration.

Example

Let's learn more about pointers through an example program, shown in Listing 2-16.

Listing 2-16. Declaring Pointers

```
var intPointer  *int           /* pointer to an integer variable */
fmt.Println("Value of intPointer: ", *intPointer)
```

In Listing 2-16, the first line declares a pointer named intPointer with int type. This is a correct way of declaration; however, if you try to print the contents of intPointer in the second line, this will throw a runtime error and the application will crash, as shown in Figure 2-9. This happens because intPointer is not currently initialized to point at anything and is hence nil.

```
>go run pointers-sample.go
panic: runtime error: invalid memory address or nil pointer dereference
[signal 0xc0000005 code=0x0 addr=0x0 pc=0x92c576]

goroutine 1 [running]:
main.main()
                        ▓▓ ▓ ▓   )/pointers-sample.go:9 +0x16
exit status 2
```

Figure 2-9. *Output of printing a nil pointer*

Let's modify Listing 2-16 to ensure that the pointer variable is pointing to a valid variable. As illustrated in Listing 2-17, we use the : = operator to explicitly declare a pointer and use the ampersand & operator to make it a pointer to another variable.

Listing 2-17. Program Showing Correct Initialization of Pointers

```
package main

import (
        "fmt"
)

func main() {
        value1 := 42
        var pointer1 = &value1
        fmt.Println("Value of pointer1: ", *pointer1)
```

41

```
        value2 := 42.13
        pointer2 := &value2
        fmt.Println("Value1: ", *pointer2)

        value3 := 32.5
        pointer3 := &value3
        *pointer3 = *pointer3 / 31
        fmt.Println("Pointer3: ", *pointer3)
        fmt.Println("Value3: ", value3)
}
```

//**Output:**

```
/*
Value of pointer1: 42
Value1: 42.13
Pointer3: 1.0483870967741935
Value3: 1.0483870967741935
*/
```

In the main function, on Line#1, we declare an integer variable with 42 as its value. On Line#2, the ampersand (&) operator is used to assign the direct memory address of the variable value1 to the variable pointer1. Since you are using an ampersand (&) operator, the Go compiler will automatically recognize that pointer1 is a pointer variable used for storing memory addresses. Now, if you print the value stored at the memory pointed by the pointer pointer1, it will be the same as that stored in value1, i.e., 42. In order to print the value stored where the memory address points, the asterisk (*) operator is used, as shown in Lines #3 and #8 of the main function. Similarly, you can use pointers to point to floating-point variables as well. Note that pointer1 is declared and assigned value implicitly, whereas the pointer2 is declared explicitly with a data type.

You can also change the values of pointed variables through the pointers, as shown in Listing 2-17:

```
*pointer1 = *pointer1 / 31
fmt.Println("Pointer1: ",*pointer1)
fmt.Println("Value1: ", value1)
```

Output:

```
Pointer3:   1.0483870967741935
Value3:   1.0483870967741935
```

On Line#1, you access the value stored at the memory location pointed by pointer1 using the asterisk (*) operator, dividing that value by 31 and storing the answer in the same location. As seen in the output, the pointer1 and value1 variables have the same value.

Comparison with Java and C-Style Languages

As in Java or C#, if you have an original variable and a reference variable (pointer) that points to that variable, you can change that value of the original variable either by changing the original variable or by changing the variable that's pointing to it. However, unlike in Java, the pointer doesn't have to point at any particular value initially, and you can change it at runtime to point to another value. On the other hand, you'll find pointers in Go to be very similar and just as valuable in C, C#, and other similar languages.

Ordered Values in Arrays and Slices

This section discusses the arrays data structure and the slice, which is an abstraction of arrays.

Arrays in Go

As with other C-style languages, Go supports the array data structure. Arrays in Go are used to store sequential fixed-size collections of elements, noticeably of the same type. Even though an array is usually referred to as a storage of a collection of items, it can also be considered a collection of variables having identical types. Furthermore, arrays are consecutive memory locations, whereby the first element of the array corresponds to the lowest address and the last element to the highest address. It is also possible to access any particular element of an array through the index number. The index numbers of an array range from 0 to size-1, as illustrated in Figure 2-10. As per the figure, to access the element in the second index (i.e., the third element), you use array_name[2], which would yield the value 11.

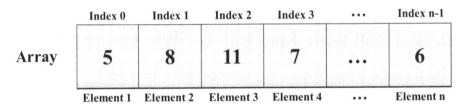

Figure 2-10. *Arrays in Go*

Declaring Arrays

The general format for declaration of an array in Go is var array_name [SIZE] data_type. Note that you must mention the data_type, as it indicates the type of elements the array will be holding. Also, the total count of elements (SIZE) is also required, as it indicates the size of the array. Arrays declared in this format are known as *single-dimensional* arrays. Note that Size should be an integer constant value that is greater than zero. Additionally, any valid Go type can be used to specify the data_type, i.e., the type of elements that the array can hold. For example, the statement var floatArray [10] float32 declares an array of ten elements called floatArray of data_type as float32.

Initializing Arrays

Arrays in Go can be initialized element at a time or using a single statement, as illustrated in Listing 2-18. Remember, the number of items specified between the curly braces { } should not exceed the size of the array specified between the square brackets [ ], as illustrated by Listing 2-18.

Listing 2-18. Initializing Arrays with Size Specified in Go

```
var floatArray = [5]float32{10.0, 200.0, 35.64, 78.0, 540.60}
```

If the size of the array is omitted, the Go compiler automatically sets the size of the array equal to the number of items specified in the initialization statement. For example, Listing 2-19 will create an array of size 5 as the array is initialized with five values.

Listing 2-19. Initializing Arrays Without Specifying Size in Go

```
var floatArray = []float32{10.0, 200.0, 35.64, 78.0, 540.60}
```

Accessing Array Elements

Individual elements of an array can be accessed through the use of indexes with array names. This is achieved by wrapping the index number of the required element within square brackets [ ], placed right after the name of the array. For example, to assign value to a single element of an array, the following statement can be used

```
balance[4] = 50.0
```

This statement assigns the value on the right side of the assignment operator to the element at the forth index of the array named `balance`. As the index number in arrays starts with 0, this statement assigns the value 50.0 to the fifth element in the array. Note, the first index of an array is also known as the *base index,* whereas the last index will always be `arraySize-1`. Also note that the = operator is used to assign values to individual elements and not the := operator, as the data type of the array has already been defined. Figure 2-11 is a pictorial representation of the concepts discussed here.

	0	1	2	3	4
balance	1000.0	2.0	3.4	7.0	50.0

Figure 2-11. *Data storage in arrays*

Example
Listing 2-20 shows an example that includes all of the concepts discussed so far.

Listing 2-20. Basic Program Illustrating the Use of Arrays in Go

```go
package main

import (
        "fmt"
)

func main(){
        /*declaring and initializing an array "array1" of
          size 3 and type as floating-point*/
        var array1 = []float32{10.5, 5.2, 2.88}

        var array2 [10]int
        var i, j int
```

```go
//Initializing elements of the array
for i =0; i < 10; i++{
    array2[i] = i + 50 //setting element at location
    i to i+50
}

//Print the value of each elements of array1
fmt.Println("Elements stored in Array1")
for j =0; j <3; j++{
    fmt.Printf("Element[%d] = %f \n", j, array1[j])
}

//Print the value of each elements of array2
fmt.Println("Elements stored in Array2)
for j =0; j <10; j++{
    fmt.Printf("Element[%d] = %d \n", j, array2[j])
}

fmt.Println("Size of array1: ", len(array1))
fmt.Println("Size of array2: ", len(array2))
}
```

/*Output:

```
$ go run array-1.go
Elements stored in Array1
Element[0] = 10.500000
Element[1] = 5.200000
Element[2] = 2.880000
Elements stored in Array1
Element[0] = 50
Element[1] = 100
Element[2] = 150
Element[3] = 200
Element[4] = 250
```

```
Element[5] = 300
Element[6] = 350
Element[7] = 400
Element[8] = 450
Element[9] = 500 */
```

Querying the Size of an Array

You can find the number of items that an array can hold (i.e., its size) by using the built-in len (short for length) function. You wrap the array identifier in the len function, like len(array_name). Listing 2-21 demonstrates the use of the len function.

Listing 2-21. Using the len Function with Array in Go

```
fmt.Println("Size of array1: ", len(array1))
fmt.Println("Size of array2: ", len(array2))
```

Output:

```
Size of array1:   3
Size of array2:   10
```

Remember that, in Go, an array is an object, and like all objects, if you pass it to a function, a copy will be made of that array. However, storing the data is just about all you can do with the arrays and it's not easy to sort or add/remove items at runtime. For such features and other operations, you should package the ordered data in slices instead of arrays.

Slices in Go

In Go, a *slice* is a layer of abstraction placed on top of the array data structure. The runtime allocates the necessary memory and constructs the array in the background when you define a slice, but only returns the slice. Furthermore, similar to arrays, all elements of a slice are of the same type. Even though arrays can simultaneously hold multiple data items of the same kind, there is no way to dynamically increase its size or extract a sub-array from it using any built-in functions. Slices get around these drawbacks. Slices are commonly utilized in Go and they provide various utility methods that are required with arrays.

Defining Slices

Slices are declared the same way as an array, with the difference that you do not specify their size, as shown in Listing 2-22. Alternatively, the make function can also be used to create slices.

Listing 2-22. Defining Slices in Go

```
var colors = []string{"ed", "Green", "Blue"}
var marks []float32            /* slice of unspecified size */
var marks = make([]int,5,5)  /* slice of length and capacity 5*/
```

The len( ) and cap( ) Functions

Being an abstraction placed on top of arrays, the underlying structure of slices are arrays. To query the total number of items present in a slice, you use the len() function. To query the total number of items that can be stored in a slice, you use the cap() function. This essentially returns the size of the slice. Listing 2-23 illustrates the use of slices in Go.

Listing 2-23. Example Illustrating the Use of the len() and cap() Functions

```
package main

import (
        "fmt"
)
```

```go
func main() {
        var marks = make([]float64, 3, 5) //declaring slice
                                          of length 3 and
                                          capacity 5
        printItemsOfSlice(marks)          //pass slice to a
                                          function
}

// function that accepts a slice and prints its details
   func printItemsOfSlice(x []float64) {
        fmt.Printf("Length=%d Capacity=%d Slice=%v\n", len(x),
        cap(x), x)
}
```

   /*Output:

s
*/

Nil Slice

A slice is initialized as nil by default if it is declared with no inputs. Also, the length and capacity of such a slice is zero. Listing 2-24 demonstrates the concept of nil slices in Go.

Listing 2-24. Nil Slices in Go

```go
package main

import "fmt"

func main() {
        var marks []float64        //declaring slice of
                                     float type
        printItemsOfSlice(marks)   //pass slice to a function
```

```go
        if marks == nil {
                fmt.Printf("Slice is Nil")
        }
}

// function that accepts a slice and prints its details
    func printItemsOfSlice(x []float64) {
        fmt.Printf("Length=%d Capacity=%d Slice=%v\n",
        len(x), cap(x), x)
}
```

/*Output:

```
Length=0 Capacity=0 Slice=[]
Slice is Nil
*/
```

Sub-Slicing in Go

In Go, you can extract a sub-slice of an array by specifying the required lower and upper bounds using [lower-bound:upper-bound]. Listing 2-25 illustrates the concept of sub-slicing in Go.

Listing 2-25. Sub-Slicing in Go

```go
package main

import "fmt"

func main() {
        /* Declare and Initialize a Slice of float type */
        marks := []float32{10, 12.6, 20.0, 37.56, 48.74, 50.0,
                64.15, 79.63, 8.75}

        /*pass slice to user-defined function to print it
        details*/
        printSliceDetails(marks)
```

```go
/* Printing the Elements of the Original Slice */
fmt.Println("Original Slice =", marks)

 /* Printing sub-slice of marks slice beginning from
     index 1(inclusive) to index 5(excluded)*/
fmt.Println("Marks[1:5] = ", marks[1:5])

/* Not indicating the lower bound inferred as 0 */
fmt.Println("Marks[:4] =", marks[:4])

/* Not indicating the upper bound is inferred as
len(slice) */
fmt.Println("Marks[3:] =", marks[3:])
marks1 := make([]float32, 0, 5)
/*pass slice to user-defined function to print it
details*/
printSliceDetails(marks1)

/* Printing sub-slice of marks beginning from
    index 0(inclusive) to index 3(exclusive) */
marks2 := marks[:3] //storing subslice in slice
                          named marks2
/*pass slice to user-defined function to print it
details*/
printSliceDetails(marks2)

/* Printing sub-slice of marks beginning from
    index 4(inclusive) to index 5(exclusive) */
marks3 := marks[4:5]
/*pass slice to user-defined function to print it
details*/
printSliceDetails(marks3)
}
```

```
func printSliceDetails(x []float32) {
        fmt.Printf("Length=%d Capacity=%d Slice=%v\n",
        len(x), cap(x), x)
}
```

/*Output:

```
Length=9 Capacity=9 Slice=[10 12.6 20 37.56 48.74 50 64.15
79.63 8.75]
Original Slice = [10 12.6 20 37.56 48.74 50 64.15 79.63 8.75]
Marks[1:5] = [12.6 20 37.56 48.74]
Marks[:4] = [10 12.6 20 37.56]
Marks[3:] = [37.56 48.74 50 64.15 79.63 8.75]
Length=0 Capacity=5 Slice=[]
Length=3 Capacity=9 Slice=[10 12.6 20]
Length=1 Capacity=5 Slice=[48.74]
*/
```

The append( ) and copy( ) Functions

In Go, the append( ) function increases the capacity of a slice. The copy( ) function copies contents of a source slice into a destination slice. Listing 2-26 shows the use of these two functions in Go.

Listing 2-26. Using the Append and Copy Functions in Go

```
package main

import "fmt"

func main() {

        /* Declaring a slice of int type */
        var nums []int

        /* pass slice to user-defined function to print details */
        printSliceDetails(nums)
```

```go
        /* Nil slice are allowed with Append */
        nums = append(nums, 10)
        printSliceDetails(nums)

        /* Adding one element to the slice */
        nums = append(nums, 100)
        printSliceDetails(nums)

        /* At one time adding more than one element to the
        slice */
        nums = append(nums, 1000, 10000, 100000)
        printSliceDetails(nums)

        /* Creating a slice nums1 that has double the capacity
        of nums slice*/
        nums1 := make([]int, len(nums), (cap(nums))*2)

        /* Copy the elements stored in nums into nums1 */
        copy(nums1, nums)

        /* pass slice to user-defined function to print
        details */
        printSliceDetails(nums1)

        var colors = []string{"Red", "Green", "Blue"}
        fmt.Println("Before: ", colors)
        colors = append(colors[1:len(colors)])
        fmt.Println("Items after removig 1st element:", colors)
}

func printSliceDetails(x []int) {
        fmt.Printf("Length=%d Capacity=%d Slice=%v\n", len(x),
        cap(x), x)
}
```

/*Output:

```
Length=0 Capacity=0 Slice=[]
Length=1 Capacity=1 Slice=[10]
Length=2 Capacity=2 Slice=[10 100]
Length=5 Capacity=6 Slice=[10 100 1000 10000 100000]
Length=5 Capacity=12 Slice=[10 100 1000 10000 100000]
*/
```

To remove items from a slice, you can also use the append() function, but this time indicate the range in the format of two numbers separated by a colon wrapped in parentheses, as shown in Listing 2-27.

Listing 2-27. Using the Append Function to Remove Items from a Slice

```
var colors = []string{"Red", "Green", "Blue"}
fmt.Println("Before: ", colors)
colors =  append(colors[1:len(colors)])
fmt.Println("Items after removing 1st element: ", colors)
```

Output:

```
Before:  [Red Green Blue]
Items after removing 1st element: [Green Blue]
```

In Listing 2-27, the first item is removed because that range is telling it to start with the item in array at index one, which is the second item.

However, in the colors = append(colors[:len(colors)-1]) statement, if the starting index in the range is eliminated and instead you pass colors[:len(colors)-1], the last item will be removed from the slice.

Sorting Slices

As shown in Listing 2-28, you can also perform sorting on slices using the sort package in Go. The sort function has multiple functions for sorting different data types. By default, the slice will be sorted in numerical order from lowest to highest using the sort() function. For more information, refer to the official developer documentation on the sort package at https://pkg.go.dev/sort. Note that, using the sort() function, you can also sort user-defined data collections.

Listing 2-28. Using Sort Function to Sort Slices

```go
package main

import (
        "fmt"
        "sort"
)

func main() {
        intSlice := make([]int, 5)
        intSlice[0] = 6
        intSlice[1] = 99
        intSlice[2] = 45
        intSlice[3] = 34
        intSlice[4] = 1

        fmt.Println("Original Slice: ", intSlice)

        sort.Ints(intSlice)

        fmt.Println("Sorted Slice: ", intSlice)
}
```

/*Output:

```
Original Slice:  [6 99 45 34 1]
Sorted Slice:   [1 6 34 45 99]
*/
```

Maps

A map, in Go language, can be considered an unordered collection of key-value pairs. In other terms, a map can be considered a hash table that allows storage of collections of data from which values can then be retrieved arbitrarily based on their keys.

Note that, as the keys are compared for sorting purposes, a map's keys should be of any type that's comparable. However, it's a usual practice of using string type for keys and any other valid type for the associated values.

Defining Maps

The make() function allocates and initializes a non-zero storage when used to declare complex data types. Therefore, it is a must to use the make() function to declare a map object. The general format for declaring a map is as follows

```
map_variable := make(map[key_data_type]value_data_type)
```

Adding Entries to a Map Object

To add an entry into the map object, use this general format: map_variable_name[key] = value. Note that because the map is an unordered collection of items, the order in which the items will be displayed is not always guaranteed.

Deleting Entries from a Map Object

In Go, to delete a map's entry (i.e., a key-value pair stored in the map), you use a built-in function called delete(). The delete() function takes two arguments—the map whose entry is to be deleted and the key to delete. The general format to achieve this is delete(map_variable, key).

Iterating Over Stored Values in a Map Object

To iterate over the key-value pairs stored in a map, you can use the For loop statement, as illustrated in Listing 2-29. Here, the key is a variable to store the keys and the value is another variable to store the corresponding value. At every iteration, the key variable will hold only one of the keys stored in the map, and the value variable will hold its corresponding value. Note that key and value are both user-defined variable names.

Listing 2-29. Using the For Loop to Iterate Over a Map

```
for key, value := range map_variable_name{
        /*perform desired operation - e.g. print all stored key-
        value pair */
        fmt.printf("%v: %v \n", key, value)
}
```

Just like the display order of a map, its iteration order is also not guaranteed. It is up to the user to manage it themselves if they want to guarantee the order. Users must list all the items stored in alphabetical order by using slices. This can be achieved by extracting the keys from the map as slices of the strings array, as illustrated in Listing 2-30.

Listing 2-30. Displaying Items of a Map

```go
package main

import (
        "fmt"
        "sort"
)

func main() {
        states := make(map[string]string)

        states["WA"] = "Washington"
        states["NY"] = "New York"
        states["CA"] = "California"

        keys := make([]string, len(states))
        i := 0
        for key := range states {
                keys[i] = key
                i++
        }

        fmt.Println("Order of Keys Before Sorting: ", keys)

        sort.Strings(keys)
        fmt.Println("Order of Keys After Forting: ", keys)
}
/*Output:

Order of Keys Before Sorting: [WA NY CA]//the display order is
                                        not guaranteed
Order of Keys After Forting: [CA NY WA]//the display order is
                                       guaranteed
*/
```

The first line declares a slice named keys of string type with a size equal to that of the map object named states. Then a for loop is used to iterate over the keys stored in the map object and store them into the keys slice. After that, to sort the keys slice, you use the sort() function that is available in the sort package. In this example, the initial key-value pairs stored in the states map were [CA:California NY:New York WA:Washington]

Using the technique shown in Listing 2-30, you can ensure that the order will be the same. Each time you iterate through a slice using the range keyword, you will get an integer representing the current index in the slice. Now you can use an integer instead to iterate over the keys slice, as shown in Listing 2-31.

Listing 2-31. Using a For Range to Iterate Over a Map

```
for i := range keys {
    fmt.Println(states[keys[i]])
    //outputs the value stored in the states map at the
    passed key
}
```

Output:

```
California
New York
Washington
```

Example

Listing 2-32 includes all of the concepts discussed previously related to how to use maps in Go to store unordered data collections in memory and then access the items arbitrarily using their keys. It also shows how to use slices and maps together to process the stored data in a desired order.

Listing 2-32. Example Illustrating the Use of Map in Go

```go
package main

import (
        "fmt"
        "sort"
)

func main() {
        states := make(map[string]string)
        fmt.Println(states)
        states["WA"] = "Washington"
        states["OR"] = "Oregon"
        states["CA"] = "California"
        fmt.Println(states)

        california := states["CA"]
        fmt.Println(california)

        delete(states, "OR")
        states["NY"] = "New York"
        fmt.Println(states)

        for key, value := range states {
                fmt.Printf("%v: %v \n", key, value)
        }

        keys := make([]string, len(states))
        i := 0
        for key := range states {
                keys[i] = key
                i++
        }
```

```
        fmt.Println(keys)
        sort.Strings(keys)
        fmt.Println(keys)

        for i := range keys {
                fmt.Println(states[keys[i]])
        }
}
```

/*Output:

```
map[]
map[CA:California OR:Oregon WA:Washington]
California
map[CA:California NY:New York WA:Washington]
WA: Washington
NY: New York
CA: California
[WA NY CA]
[CA NY WA]
California
New York
Washington
*/
```

Structs Data Type

As discussed earlier, arrays in Go are essentially variables that can store multiple data items of the *same* kind. To overcome this limitation, Go offers *structures,* which are user-defined types that can be used to store data items of *different* kinds. A structure essentially represents a *record* of data. For example, if there is a need to track different information about books available in a library, structures are the most useful way to store different attributes of a book, such as BookID, Title, Subject, Author, and so on.

Defining a Structure

To define a structure, you must use the type and struct statements. The struct statement defines a new data type that will contain multiple members. The type statement binds a name to the structure. The general format for declaring a structure using the type and struct statements is illustrated in Listing 2-33.

Listing 2-33. General Format for Declaring Structures in Go

```
type struct_variable_type struct {
   member definition;
   member definition;
   ...
   member definition;
}
```

After defining a structure type in your code, multiple variables of this struct type can be declared. The general format for doing so is variable_name := structure_variable_type {value1, value2...value n}

Accessing Members of a Structure

In order to access any member field of a struct, you use the member access operator (.). Remember that the struct keyword is mandatory for defining variables of a defined struct type. Listing 2-34 illustrates the use of the struct type in Go and shows how to access its member fields.

Listing 2-34. Using Structs in Go

```go
package main

import "fmt"

type Books struct {
        bTitle      string
        bAuthorName string
        bSubject    string
        book_id     int
}

func main() {
        var Book1 Books /* Declaring variable of type Book */
        var Book2 Books /* Declaring variable of type Book */

        /* Access member fields of Book struct to define Book1 */
        Book1.bTitle = "The Go Programming Language"
        Book1.bAuthorName = "Alan A. A. Donovan and Brian
        W. Kernighan"
        Book1.bSubject = "A complete guide to Go programming"
        Book1.book_id = 6495

        /* Access member fields of Book struct to define Book2 */
        Book2.bTitle = "The Complete Book of Arts & Crafts"
        Book2.bAuthorName = "Dawn Purney"
        Book2.bSubject = "The Complete Book of Arts and Crafts
        of fun activities for children"
        Book2.book_id = 6496

        /* Print the details of Book1 */
        fmt.Printf("Book1 bTitle : %s\n", Book1.bTitle)
        fmt.Printf("Book1 bAuthorName : %s\n", Book1.bAuthorName)
```

```
    fmt.Printf("Book1 bSubject : %s\n", Book1.bSubject)
    fmt.Printf("Book1 book_id : %d\n", Book1.book_id)

    /* Print the details of Book1 */
    fmt.Printf("Book2 bTitle : %s\n", Book2.bTitle)
    fmt.Printf("Book2 bAuthorName : %s\n", Book2.bAuthorName)
    fmt.Printf("Book2 bSubject : %s\n", Book2.bSubject)
    fmt.Printf("Book2 book_id : %d\n", Book2.book_id)
}
```

/*Output:

```
Book1 bTitle      : The Go Programming Language
Book1 bAuthorName : Alan A. A. Donovan and Brian W. Kernighan
Book1 bSubject    : A complete guide to Go programming
Book1 book_id     : 6495

Book2 bTitle      : The Complete Book of Arts & Crafts
Book2 bAuthorName : Dawn Purney
Book2 bSubject    : The Complete Book of Arts and Crafts of fun
                    activities for children
Book2 book_id     : 6496
*/
```

Passing Structures as Function Arguments

In Go, just like with any other variable or pointer, you can also pass a structure as a function argument. Listing 2-35 illustrates how to pass structures as function arguments.

Listing 2-35. Passing Structures as Function Arguments in Go

```go
package main

import "fmt"

type Books struct {
        bTitle      string
        bAuthorName string
        bSubject    string
        book_id     int
}

func main() {
        var Book1 Books /* Declaring variable of type Book */
        var Book2 Books /* Declaring variable of type Book */

        /* Access member fields of Book struct to define Book1 */
        Book1.bTitle = "The Go Programming Language"
        Book1.bAuthorName = "Alan A. A. Donovan and Brian
        W. Kernighan"
        Book1.bSubject = "A complete guide to Go programming"
        Book1.book_id = 6495

        /* Access member fields of Book struct to define Book2 */
        Book2.bTitle = "The Complete Book of Arts & Crafts"
        Book2.bAuthorName = "Dawn Purney"
        Book2.bSubject = "The Complete Book of Arts and Crafts
        of fun activities for children"
        Book2.book_id = 6496

        /* Print the details of Book1 by passing it as an
        argument to function */
        printBookDetails(Book1)
```

```
        /* Print the details of Book2 by passing it as an
        argument to function */
        printBookDetails(Book2)
}

func printBookDetails(book Books) {
        fmt.Printf("\nTitle : %s\n", book.bTitle)
        fmt.Printf("Authors : %s\n", book.bAuthorName)
        fmt.Printf("Subject : %s\n", book.bSubject)
        fmt.Printf("Book ID : %d\n", book.book_id)
}
```

/*Output:

```
Title   : The Go Programming Language
Authors : Alan A. A. Donovan and Brian W. Kernighan
Subject : A complete guide to Go programming
Book ID : 6495

Title   : The Complete Book of Arts & Crafts
Authors : Dawn Purney
Subject : The Complete Book of Arts and Crafts of fun
          activities for children
Book ID : 6496
*/
```

Pointers to Structures

Just as you can define pointers that can be used for pointing (storing) to other constants or variables, you can also define pointers to structures in Go. For example, a pointer variable named struct_pointer of the type Books can be declared using the var struct_pointer *Books statement. The struct_pointer variable can then be used to store addresses of structure variables. The ampersand (&) operator gets the direct address of a structure variable, for example, struct_pointer = &Book1. Furthermore, the member access operator (.) accesses the members of a structure where the pointer is pointing, such as struct_pointer.title

Example

Let's rewrite Listing 2-35 to illustrate the use of structure pointers in Go. The result is shown in Listing 2-36.

Listing 2-36. Program to Illustrate Structure Pointers in Go

```go
package main

import "fmt"

type Books struct {
        bTitle     string
        bAuthorName string
        bSubject   string
        book_id    int
}

func main() {
        var Book1 Books /* Declaring variable of type Book */
        var Book2 Books /* Declaring variable of type Book */

        /* Access member fields of Book struct to define Book1 */
        Book1.bTitle = "The Go Programming Language"
        Book1.bAuthorName = "Alan A. A. Donovan and Brian
        W. Kernighan"
        Book1.bSubject = "A complete guide to Go programming"
        Book1.book_id = 6495

        /* Access member fields of Book struct to define Book2 */
        Book2.bTitle = "The Complete Book of Arts & Crafts"
        Book2.bAuthorName = "Dawn Purney"
```

```
        Book2.bSubject = "The Complete Book of Arts and Crafts
                        of fun activities for children"
        Book2.book_id = 6496

        /* Print the details of Book1 by passing it as a
        pointer to function */
        printBookDetails(&Book1)

        /* Print the details of Book2 by passing it as a
        pointer to function */
        printBookDetails(&Book2)
}

func printBookDetails(book *Books) {
        fmt.Printf("\nTitle : %s\n", book.bTitle)
        fmt.Printf("Authors : %s\n", book.bAuthorName)
        fmt.Printf("Subject : %s\n", book.bSubject)
        fmt.Printf("Book ID : %d\n", book.book_id)
}
```

   /***Output:**

```
Title   : The Go Programming Language
Authors : Alan A. A. Donovan and Brian W. Kernighan
Subject : A complete guide to Go programming
Book ID : 6495

Title   : The Complete Book of Arts & Crafts
Authors : Dawn Purney
Subject : The Complete Book of Arts and Crafts of fun
          activities for children
Book ID : 6496
*/
```

The struct type in Go is a data structure that has similar purpose and function as the struct type in C and as classes in Java. Structs can encapsulate data and methods. However, unlike Java, Go does not have an inheritance model, that is, there is no concept of a super() function or substructures. Each structure is independent with its own fields for data management and optionally its own methods. Remember that struct in Go is a custom type. Note that the structure name starts with a capital letter, e.g., Book, to ensure that it can be used in other parts of the applications, i.e., exported, similar to public access specifiers in C-style languages. On the other hand, if a lowercase initial character is used, the struct type will be private and cannot be exported for use in other parts of the application.

Program Flow

Conditional logic can be used to change the program flow. Like other C-style languages, Go also offers conditional statements like if, if…else, nested if, switch, and select. However, there is a slight syntax difference in their uses.

If Statement

For most of the part, the if statement in Go looks the same as in C or Java; however, it does not need parentheses around the Boolean condition. Another important aspect is how you format your conditional code blocks. In other C-style languages, there is the option available of starting your beginning brace of a code block on the next line. This is not the case with Go, and doing so will throw an error. The opening brace has to be on the same line as the preceding statement. Listing 2-37 is an example of using an if-else statement is Go.

Listing 2-37. Illustration of an if-else Statement in Go

```go
package main

import (
        "fmt"
)

func main() {
        theAnswer := 42
        var result string

        if theAnswer < 0 {
                result = "Less than Zero"
        } else if theAnswer == 0 {
                result = "Equal to Zero"
        } else {
                result = "Greater than Zero"
        }

        fmt.Println(result)
}

    /*Output:

Greater than Zero
*/
```

Another interesting and sometimes useful variation in Go's if syntax is that you can include an initial statement that's part of the if statement. For example, you can initialize a variable before performing conditional logic based on its value. Listing 2-38 is an example of doing this.

Listing 2-38. An if Statement with Initialization

```
if x:= 50; if x < 0 {
      result = "Less than Zero"
} else if x == 0 {
      result = "Equal to Zero"
} else {
      result = "Greater than Zero"
}
fmt.Println(result)
```

Output:

```
Greater than Zero
```

Switch Statement

Like other C-Style languages, the Go language also offers switch statements that serve the same purpose; however their syntax expands on those languages. A switch statement can be used on a variable to test a variable's equality against a list of values. Listing 2-39 uses the Math. Rand package from the rand package; we will be using the seed() function and passing it the current time in UNIX format using the statement rand. seed(time.Now().Unix()). Next, the Intn() function from the rand package returns a non-negative pseudo-random integer. The Intn() function requires you to specify a range interval [0,n). It is important to make sure that n <= 0. In this example, we provided a ceiling value of 7+1, i.e., the function will use the interval [0, 7) + 1. In this way the function will return a number between one and seven. Each time you run this application, it will generate a different number depending on the millisecond of the current time on your computer. (It is possible to see the same number again and again, but that's just a coincidence.) Every time the code in Listing 2-39 runs, you will possibly get different output.

Listing 2-39. Using a switch Statement in Go

```go
package main

import (
        "fmt"
        "math/rand"
        "time"
)

func main() {
        rand.Seed(time.Now().Unix())
        dow := rand.Intn(7) + 1
        fmt.Println("Day: ", dow)

        var result string
        switch dow {
        case 1:
                result = "It's Sunday"
        case 2:
                result = "It's Monday"
        default:
                result = "It's some other day"
        }

        fmt.Println(result)
}
```

Output:

```
Day:  2
It's Monday
```

Note that in the switch statement, the parentheses are not required around the expression that is being evaluated. One more difference from C and Java is that the switch statement in Go does not require the break

73

statement. In Go, as soon as one of the cases is evaluated as true, the
statements within that case are executed and the control is transferred to
the end of the switch statement. Furthermore, just like the if statement,
you can also include a short statement before the evaluation of the
variables in the switch statement, as shown in Listing 2-40. Remember
that any variable declared in the switch statement will be local to that
switch statement.

Listing 2-40. Using a Switch Statement with Evaluation Statement

```go
package main
import (
        "fmt"
        "math/rand"
        "time"
)

func main() {
        rand.Seed(time.Now().Unix())
        var result string

        switch dow := rand.Intn(7) + 1; dow {
        case 1:
                result = "It's Sunday"
        case 2:
                result = "It's Monday"
        default:
                result = "It's some other day"
        }

        fmt.Println(result)
}
```

In Go, the `fallthrough` keyword is used in the `case` block of the `switch` statement. If the `fallthrough` keyword is present in any `case` block, it will transfer the program's control flow to the next case, whether or not the current case evaluated to `true`.

For Statement

Unlike the other high-level programming languages, Go offers only one looping construct, namely the `for` loop. The `for` loop can be used for repetitive tasks such as iterating through collections of values. The basic syntax of the `for` loop is identical to that in Java or C-style languages, with the exception that the parentheses ( ) in the `for` statement are not required. Furthermore, just like C-style languages or Java, the pre- and post- statements in the `for` loop statement are not mandatory and can be left blank. Additionally, in Go, a `for` loop can be used in four variations, discussed here:

1. **A `for` loop with step variable, condition, and range.**

   The `range` keyword is used in Go to iterate over elements stored in a variety of data structures. When used with arrays and slices, the `range` keyword also returns the index and value for each entry. In Listing 2-41, in the second `for` loop, we used the blank identifier (_) to ignore the index. However, as in the third `for` loop, the indexes are sometimes required as well. In the fourth `for` loop, the range will return to the variable i from a comma-delimited list. The first variable will be the index and the second will be the associated value.

Listing 2-41. For Loop with Step Variable, Condition, and Range

```go
package main

import "fmt"

func main() {
    total := 0
    for k := 0; k < 5; k++ {
        total += k
    }

    nums := []int{2, 3, 4}
    total = 0
    for _, num := range nums {
        total += num
    }

    fmt.Println("Total:", total)

    for j, num := range nums {
        if num == 2 {
            fmt.Println("Index:", j)
        }
    }

    for i := range nums {
        fmt.Println(nums[i])
    }
}
```

Output:

```
Total: 9
Index: 0
2
3
4
```

2. **A** for **loop with blank pre/post statements**

   Listing 2-42 illustrates the use of for loops with blank pre/post statements.

Listing 2-42. For Loop with Blank Pre/Post Statements

```
total := 1
for ; total < 10; {
    total += total
}
```

3. **A** for **loop as a** while **loop**

   Many languages have a while keyword that lets you loop over a set of statement(s) as long as a Boolean expression is true. Go implements this type of looping using the for keyword. Instead of a counter variable or a range, you just declare a Boolean condition. Listing 2-43 illustrates this concept.

Listing 2-43. Using a For Loop as a While Loop

```
total := 1
for  < 10 {
   total += total
}
```

4. **Infinite loop**

    In general, if the specified condition statement
    of a loop never turns false, the loop turns into an
    infinite loop. Usually, for loops are used for creating
    infinite loops. When all of the three expressions in
    the for statement are not specified, this makes the
    condition statement remain true forever, turning the
    for loop into an infinite loop. Listing 2-44 illustrates
    this concept.

Listing 2-44. Using a For loop as an Inifinite Loop

```
for {
    // Any task you want to loop forever
}
```

The goto Statement

Go also supports the goto statement, which transfers control to a label in
the code. Listing 2-45 illustrates the use of labels with goto statements to
alter the program control flow. In this snippet, when the if statement turns
true, the goto statement will be executed and control will be·transferred to
the theEnd label, then the statements following this label will be executed.
Listing 2-45 illustrates a basic program depicting the use of a goto
statement in Go.

Listing 2-45. Using the goto Statement in Go

```
package main

import (
        "fmt"
)
```

```go
func main() {
        total := 1
        for total < 5 {
                total += total
                fmt.Println("Total: ", total)
                if total == 5 {
                        goto theEnd
                }
        }
theEnd:
        fmt.Println("End of Program")
}
```

Output:

```
Total:  2
Total:  4
Total:  8
End of Program
```

To summarize, Go supports the use of continue, break, and goto statements. Go also supports looping with a variety of coding patterns and adds features to the for statement to make it concise and readable.

Functions

Go is organized into packages and packages have functions. Every Go application has a package named main and at least one function, also named main. The main function is called automatically by the runtime as the application starts up. In Go, like other programming languages, you can also create custom functions and organize them into your own custom packages.

A function declaration tells the Go compiler what the function name is, its return type, and the input parameters. On the other hand, the function definition is the actual body of the function and is a set of the statement(s) that perform the intended task.

Several built-in functions are provided by the Go standard library that you can call and use in your Go programs. For example, the len() function takes arguments of various types as input and returns their length. Functions are also called methods, subroutines, or procedures.

Defining a Function

A function definition in Go is made up of two parts—the function header and the body. The general format for defining a function in Go is shown in Listing 2-46.

Listing 2-46. General Format of Functions in Go

```
func function_name( [parameter list] ) [return_types]
{
   body of the function
}
```

Here, the func keyword instructs the compiler about the start of a function declaration and function_name represents the function's name. Function signature is referred to as the function's name and input parameter list combined. Also, parameters are used as placeholders. Values passed to the function when it is invoked are called function arguments and these parameters are also referred to as formal parameters. A function's parameter list defines the type, order, and total count parameters it will take as input. It is possible that a function may have no parameters and hence the parameters are optional. return_type is used to define the data type of value(s) the function may return. Here again, the return_type is optional if the function does not return anything. The body of the function contains multiple statements that together define the task it has to perform.

Listing 2-47 illustrates the use of custom functions in Go. Here, findMaximum() is a user-defined function that takes two parameters, n1 and n2. As output, it returns the maximum value among the two passed values. Also, because both the parameters are of the same type, it is not necessary to specify the type with each variable.

Listing 2-47. Basic Program Illustrating Custom Functions in Go

```go
/* Function to find maximum value among two numbers */
func findMaximum(n1, n2 int) int {
        /* Declaring Local Variables */
        var maxVal int

        if (n1 > n2) {
          maxVal = n1
        } else {
            maxVal = n2
        }
        return maxVal
}
```

Like other languages, Go functions can also accept an arbitrary number of values of the same type. To do this, as shown in Listing 2-48, you declare the parameter name, then add three dots, and then specify the data type. As values will act as an array, the range keyword can be used to loop over the values stored in it.

Listing 2-48. Functions with Arbitrary Number of Values

```go
package main

import (
        "fmt"
)

func main() {
        total := addValues(40, 50, 60)
        fmt.Println("Sum of Passed Values: ", total)
}

func addValues(values ... int) int{
        sum := 0
        for _, val := range values{
                sum += val
        }
        return sum
}
```

   /*Output:

```
Sum of Passed Values:   150
*/
```

Doing Function Calls in Go

In order to create a function in Go, it is necessary to provide its definition
as well, which defines what task the function should perform. In order to
use a function, it has to be called from the program. When a function call is
made from a program, the control flow is transferred to it. When the called
function finishes the defined task or a return statement is encountered or
the closing brace of the function is reached, the control flow returns to the
program where the initial call was made.

To make a function call, you simply pass the required parameters, wrapped within parentheses () next to the function name. If a value is to be returned from the function, the returned values can either be used directly, like with Println(), or can be stored and reused later for performing different operations. Listing 2-49 illustrates the concept of performing function calls in Go.

Listing 2-49. Basic Program to Illustrate Function Calls in Go

```go
package main

import "fmt"

func main() {
    /* Defining Local Variables */
    var val1 int = 50
    var val2 int = 80
    var retVal int

    /* Function call to findMaximum() */
    retVal = findMaximum(val1, val2)

    fmt.Printf("Maximum value: %d\n", retVal)
}

/* Function to find maximum value between the two numbers */
func findMaximum(num1, num2 int) int {

    /* Declaring Local Variables */
    var maxVal int

    if (num1 > num2) {
        maxVal = num1
    } else {
        maxVal = num2
    }
```

```
    return maxVal
}
```

Output:

```
Maximum Value: 80
```

Return More than One Value from Functions

Unlike other C-style languages, Go functions are designed to return multiple values at a time. The following example illustrates how to return values from a function. Refer to the official documentation at https:// golangdocs.com/functions-in-golang to learn more ways of returning values and syntax variations in Go. Listing 2-50 illustrates this concept.

Listing 2-50. Go Program Illustrating How to Return More than One Value from Functions

```
package main

import (
    "fmt"
)

func swapValues(str1, str2 string) (string, string) {
    return str2, str1
}
func main() {
    val1, val2 := swapValues("Abdullah", "Hassan")
    fmt.Println("Values After Swap: ", val1, val2)
}
```

Output:

```
"Values After Swap: Hassan Abdullah
```

Passing Arguments to Functions

You must declare all of the variables that would accept the values passed to the function as its arguments. This set of variables are also known as a function's formal parameters. Note that the scope of all of the formal parameters of a function is local to it only, i.e., they are accessible only within the scope of that particular function. Furthermore, the formal parameters are only created upon entering the function and are destroyed when it exits.

There are two ways to pass arguments to a function—*call by value* and *call by reference*. When the call by value way of passing arguments is used, it basically copies the value of the passed argument into the formal parameters of the called function. Any changes made to the formal parameters inside the respective function have no effect on the value of the argument that was passed with function call.

On the other hand, the call by reference technique copies the direct address of the passed argument into the formal parameters of the called function. As the direct address is copied and used to access the actual argument, any changes made to the formal parameters inside the respective function will also be reflected in the argument passed with the function call. To ensure that a function cannot change the value of the passed arguments, by default, call by value is used to pass arguments to functions in the Go programming language.

Call by Value Example

Listing 2-51 illustrates the concept of call by value in Go.

Listing 2-51. Go Program Showing Call by Value

```
package main

import (
        "fmt"
)
```

```go
func modifyInt(val int) int {
    return val + 5
}

func main() {
    num := 500
    fmt.Println("Value of Passed Argument
                Before Function Call: ", num)

    fmt.Println("Value Returned by Function call:",
                modifyInt(num))

    fmt.Println("Value of Passed Argument
                After Function Call: ", num)
}
```

Output:

```
Value of Passed Argument Before Function Call:   500
Value Returned by Function call: 505
Value of Passed Argument After Function Call:   500
```

Call by Reference Example

Listing 2-52 illustrates the concept of call by reference in Go.

Listing 2-52. Go Program Illustrating Call by Reference in Go

```go
package main

import (
        "fmt"
)
```

```go
func myMap(mapObject map[int]int) {
        //make() declares as well as initializes the map to 0
        mapObject = make(map[int]int)
}

func myInt(values []int) {
        //make() declares as well as initializes the slice to 0
        values = make([]int, 5)
}

func main() {
        //mapObject is declared but NOT initialized, i.e., its
        value is nil
        var mapObject map[int]int
        myMap(mapObject)
        fmt.Println("Is the map equal to nil? ",
        mapObject == nil)

        //Slice is declared but NOT initialized, i.e., its
        value is nil
        var intSlice []int
        myInt(intSlice)
        fmt.Println("Is the slice equal to nil? ",
        intSlice == nil)
}
```

Output:

```
Is the map equal to nil?  true
Is the slice equal to nil?  true
```

Methods

In Go, if functions are attached to user-defined custom types, they are then referred to as methods. In the case of an object-oriented language like Java, each method is a member of a class. Whereas, in Go a method is a member of a type. Listing 2-53 illustrates how to attach a method to the struct.

Listing 2-53. Example Illustrating the Use of Methods in Go

```go
package main

import (
        "fmt"
)

func main() {
        poodle := Dog{"Poodle", 10, "woff!"}
        fmt.Println(poodle)
        fmt.Printf("%+v\n", poodle)
        fmt.Printf("Breed: %v\nWeight: %v \n", poodle.Breed,
        poodle.Weight)

        poodle.Speak()
}

//Dog is a struct
type Dog struct {
        Breed  string
        Weight int
        Sound  string
}

func (d Dog) Speak() {
        fmt.Println(d.Sound)
}
```

/*Output:

```
{Poodle 10 woff!}
{Breed: Poodle Weight:10 Sound:woff!}
Breed: Poodle
Weight: 10
woff!
*/
```

Go doesn't support method overriding; each method must have its own unique name. But like all functions, methods can return values just to clear the type assigned to the method, as shown in Listing 2-54.

Listing 2-54. Methods with Returning Values

```go
package main

import (
        "fmt"
)

func main() {
        poodle := Dog{"Poodle", 10, "woff!"}
        fmt.Println(poodle)
        fmt.Printf("%+v\n", poodle)
        fmt.Printf("Breed: %v\nWeight: %v \n", poodle.Breed,
        poodle.Weight)

        poodle.Speak()
        poodle.Sound = "Arf!"
        poodle.Speak()
        poodle.SpeakThreeTimes()
}
```

```go
//Dog is a struct
type Dog struct {
        Breed   string
        Weight int
        Sound   string
}

func (d Dog) Speak() {
        fmt.Println(d.Sound)
}

func (d Dog) SpeakThreeTimes() {
        d.Sound = fmt.Sprintf("%v %v %v", d.Sound, d.Sound,
        d.Sound)
        fmt.Println(d.Sound)
}
```

   /*Output:

```
{Poodle 10 woff!}
{Breed:Poodle Weight:10 Sound:woff!}
Breed: Poodle
Weight: 10
Woff!
Arf!
Arf! Arf! Arf!
*/
```

Note that when you pass the dog object to a function as the receiver, a copy is made of it, i.e. this is pass by value and not reference. If you want it to be a reference, you can use pointers. But within the function, this is a brand new copy of the object. So when you modify the sound field, you are not modifying the version that was created in the main function. The ability to create custom methods for your own types makes the Go programming language behave more like a fully object-oriented language. Even without the sort of type inheritance that you find in C++ and Java, a struct can have as many different methods as it needs to accomplish your application's requirements.

Write/Read Text Files

There are a number of ways to create a file in Go. There are high-level abstractions of the low-level operations that are required.

Write Text Files

The example in Listing 2-55 shows you how to write to a file in Go. The checkError() will be used for error checking throughout this program. The function will check the object passed to it and if the object is not nil, i.e., an error has occurred performing some operation in the main program, the function will crash the application and display the error message.

In the main() function, the content variable holds the string value you want to write to the fromString.txt file. On Line#2, in the main() function, we create a file reference named file, which is basically a variable that will be used as a reference to the file. Along with this, we also specify a variable called err to store error messages returned by the os. Create() function. The Create() function takes the location of the file to which the data should be written. Furthermore, it creates the named file if it doesn't exist or truncates it if it already exists. Here, the ./ means the file is in the same directory as the application.

On Line#4 in the main() function, the length variable stores the number of bytes written to the file as returned by the WriteString() function. The WriteString() function requires a writer object and a string, here we passed file as the writer and the content variable as the string that has to be written to the file. Whenever you're working with files, it is of utmost importance to close files that you opened when you are done. The defer keyword is waiting until everything else is done and then executes this command. With the defer keyword, we have written the file.Close() command to ensure that when everything is done, the file referred to in the file reference object is closed.

Listing 2-55. Program Illustrating How to Write to Text Files in Go

```go
package main

import (
        "fmt"
        "io"
        "io/ioutil"
)

func main() {
        content := "Hello from Go! "
        file, err := os.Create("./fromString.txt")
        checkError(err)
        defer file.Close()
        length, err := io.WriteString(file, content)
        checkError(err)
        fmt.Printf("Wrote a file with %v characters\n",length)
}

/* checkError is a function for error checking */
func checkError(err error) {
        if err != nil {
                panic(err)
        }

}
```

Output:

```
Wrote a file with 14 characters
```

fromString.txt - Notepad

File   Edit   Format   View   Help
```
Hello from Go!
```

Read Text Files

In this section, in order to illustrate how reading data from a text file can be achieved in Go, as shown in Listing 2-56, we modify the previous example in Listing 2-55 by adding a custom function called readFile() which will take a filename as input. Whenever a file is read, it is always returned as an array of bytes. The data variable in Listing 2-56 will hold the returned bytes. Once again, the err object checks if an error is thrown. The ReadFile() function is a built-in function in the ioutil package that can be used to read any file indicated by the filename passed to it as an argument. As output, it returns the contents of the file read. Upon successful execution of the ReadFile(), the error value is returned as nil instead of EOF. This is because the ReadFile() function reads as input the entire file and does not treat an EOF returned from the Read() function as an error. At the last line in the readFile(), the string(data) statement is used to type-cast the contents of the file received as bytes into the string to display them on the screen. In the main() function we used the defer keyword again and then called the readFile() function and passed it the file we want to read. It is important to use the defer keyword whenever you are working with anything that might not run automatically in the current thread. Also, if you want to wait until the file is completely closed before you try to read it, the defer keyword achieves this for you.

Listing 2-56. Reading from Text Files in Go

```go
package main

import (
        "fmt"
        "io"
        "io/ioutil"
        "os"
)

func main() {
        content := "Hello from Go!"
        file, err := os.Create("./fromString.txt")
        checkError(err)
        length, err := io.WriteString(file, content)
        checkError(err)
        fmt.Printf("Wrote a file with %v characters\n", length)
        readFile(file.Name())
        defer file.Close()
}

// readFile is a function for reading content of text file
func readFile(fileName string) {
        data, err := ioutil.ReadFile(fileName)
        checkError(err)
        fmt.Println("Text read from file: ", string(data))
}

// checkError is a function for error checking
func checkError(err error) {
        if err != nil {
                panic(err)
        }
}
```

Output:

```
Wrote a file with 14 characters
Hello from Go!
```

HTTP Package

To help programmers build applications that can effectively communicate with different web applications and services, the Go programming language offers an extensive set of different tools, one of them being the http package. The http package allows you to easily communicate with remote hosts by creating requests and sending data. It also helps in creating HTTP server applications that can listen and respond to the received requests. The example in Listing 2-57 illustrates the use of the http package.

In Listing 2-57, a request is sent to a remote host to fetch some data. Here, we want to download the JSON contents of the page specified in the content named url to the local development machine. To do so, the first step is to import the net/http and ioutil packages. To download the content use the get() function from the http package. The get() function returns a response object as well as an error object. The resp variable is used to store the returned response object. When you print the contents of the resp variable, you will get a pointer to an object named response. Notice that it's a member of the http package. The response object has a public field called body. It contains the JSON packet you intend to download. Just like with files, after reading the contents of the body, you should use the defer keyword along with the resp.Body.Close() command to close the body.

The contents are received in the form of a byte array. To store this, use the bytes variable. The ioutil.ReadAll(resp.Body) reads the contents of the resp.Body. Since the returned content is a byte array, you have to type-cast it into a string to print it onto the screen, by wrapping the bytes variable within the string type using the string(bytes) command.

Listing 2-57. Basic Program Showing the Use of the HTTP
Package in Go

```go
package main

import (
        "fmt"
        "io/ioutil"
        "net/http"
)

const url = "http://services.explorecalifornia.org/json/
            tours.php"

func main() {
        fmt.Println("Network Requests Demo")

        response, err := http.Get(url)

        if err != nil {
                panic(err)
        }
        fmt.Printf("Response Type: %T\n", response)

        defer response.Body.Close()

        bytes, err := ioutil.ReadAll(response.Body)
        if err != nil {
                panic(err)
        }
        content := string(bytes)
        fmt.Print(content)
}
```

Output:

>go run http-sample.go
Network Requests Demo
Response Type: *http.Response
[{"tourId":"14","packageId":"5","packageTitle":"From Desert to Sea","name":"2 Days Adrift the Salton Sea","blurb":"The Salton Sea, 25% saltier than the Pacific, has bee
n a tourist destination since the 1920s. See what attracts people to this desert oasis.","description":"The Salton Sea is saltier than the Pacific, an unusual feat for
inland body of water. And even though its salinity has risen over the years, due in part to lack of outflows and pollution from agricultural runoff, it has attracted a
small, but dedicated population. The sea itself offers recreational opportunities including boating, camping, off-roading, hiking, use of personal watercraft, photograp
hy and bird watching. The sea has been termed a \"crown jewel of avian biodiversity,\" being a major resting stop on the Pacific Flyway, a migratory path for birds. 2 D
ays Adrift the Salton Sea includes two nights accommodations at the Bombay Beach Inn, boat rental at the Salton City Harbor, and a guided fishing tour.","price":"150","
difficulty":"2","length":"2","graphic":"map_saltonsea.gif","region":"Southern California"},{"tourId":"26","packageId":"9","packageTitle":"Taste of California","name":"A
Week of Wine","blurb":"Spend a week in wine country. Watch the evolution of a wine from harvesting to corking. In the heart of Sonoma Valley, considered the birthplace
of wine-making in California. ","description":"Immerse yourself in the culture and lifestyle of a California winery. Spend 5 days in your private guest villa at the St
ockbridge Winery, located in scenic Sonoma. You'll spend your days wandering the vineyards, touring the presses and cellars, and assisting staff in making America's fav
orite wine. Enjoy Tuscan-style meals served al fresco, overlooking the gorgeous countryside. Day trips include dinner in Sausalito, hiking in the redwood forests, and l
unch in downtown San Francisco.","price":"850","difficulty":"Easy","length":"5","graphic":"map_winecountry.gif","region":"Napa\/Sonoma Counties"},{"tourId":"11","packag
eId":"4","packageTitle":"Cycle California","name":"Amgen Tour of California Special","blurb":"This year only, we\u2019re also offering a special package that allows ser
ious cyclists to follow behind a competitor in the AMGEN bike race, a race that mimics the conditions in the Tour de France. Spots are limited so reserve your seat now!
","description":"The AMGEN Tour of California is the largest cycling event in the US, over 750 miles and includes cycling world champions, Tour de France competitors, a
nd Olympic athletes. It's an 8-leg tour, designed to mimic the various conditions in the Tour de Trance, and Explore California has the unique pleasure of being able to
offer 50 of our members spots behind the peloton, or main group of racers, on two legs of the two. This is a special, one-time only offer. Customers should be in physi
cal and mental shape to complete this two-week ride. Be prepared to complete a detailed questionnaire about skill level and any existing health problems.","price":"6000
","difficulty":"Difficult","length":"14","graphic":"map_northerncal.gif","region":"Northern California"},{"tourId":"9","packageId":"3","packageTitle":"California Hotspr
ings","name":"Avila Beach Hot springs","blurb":"Spend a weekend in a rustic log cabin, within walking distance of the historic Avila Hot Springs and minutes from the be
ach.","description":"\"Chumash have occupied Avila Beach for centuries, but it wasn't until the late 19th century that the rest of California realized its ideal climate
, proximity to the ocean and artesian springs made Avila Beach an ideal resort town. The hot springs in Avila are really unique, creating pools that hover at a natural
104 degrees, which draws aficionados from far and wide. You'll stay at the historic Avila Hot Springs Resort, situated between oak-covered foothills that keep the morn
ing fog away and make a natural year round air conditioner, which will enhance a nice morning, afternoon, or evening swim. This package include a two night stay in a pr
ivate cabin above the springs, and a 3 day pass to the fresh water pool and 400 sq feet hot mineral pool. Optional day trips include two hour kayaking tours (we love th
e Cave Expedition) from Central Coast Kayaks and docent-led trips from the Point San Luis Lighthouse down the Pechos Trail. \"","price":"1000","difficulty":"Easy","leng
th":"3","graphic":"map_avilabeach.gif","region":"Central Coast"},{"tourId":"1","packageId":"1","packageTitle":"Backpack Cal","name":"Big Sur Retreat","blurb":"Big Sur i
s big country. The Big Sur Retreat takes you to the most majestic part of the Pacific Coast and show you the secret trails.","description":"\"The region know as Big Sur
is like Yosemite's younger cousin, with all the redwood scaling, rock climbing and, best of all, hiking that the larger park has to offer. Robison Jeffers once said, \
"\"Big Sur is the greatest meeting of land and sea in the world,\"\" but the highlights are only accessible on foot. Our 3-day tour allows you to choose from multiple h
ikes led by experienced guides during the day, while comfortably situated in the evenings at the historic Big Sur River Inn. Take a tranquil walk to the coastal waterfa
ll at Julia Pfeiffer Burns State Par or hike to the Harried Redwoods. If you're prepared for a more strenuous climb, try Ollason's Peak in Toro Park. An optional 4th da
y Includes admission to the Henry Miller Library and the Point Reyes Lighthouse.\"","price":"750","difficulty":"Medium","length":"3","graphic":"map_bigsur.gif","region"
:"Central Coast"},{"tourId":"5","packageId":"1","packageTitle":"Backpack Cal","name":"Channel Islands Excursion","blurb":"The chain known as the Channel Islands offer s
one of the most diverse and unique landscape on the Pacific coast. No motor vehicles are allowed on the islands, which makes this daytrip hiking package the best and mo
st interesting way to visit.","description":"The Channel Islands Excursion starts with a ferry from beautiful Ventura to the nearest island in the strand, Santa Cruz. Y

JSON

The data returned as a response to a request made to a web service is commonly encoded in the JSON format. To facilitate working with web services and APIs, Go offers support for handling JSON-formatted data in the form of the json package. The json package allows you to easily create and read text that is in the JSON format. In the previous section, you learned how to get JSON data from a web service. In this section, you learn how to parse the JSON data and format it into structured data for use in your Go applications. Listing 2-58 is a demonstration of how to parse JSON data and format it into structured data. It parses the tour name and price from the received JSON data.

In Listing 2-58, you first create a new custom type named Tour, which will be a struct with two member fields of string type—Name and Price. Note that to make these field names public, they start with an uppercase character. Also note that in the JSON content the labels are all in lowercase. However, the JSON decoder is not affected by this, as it can easily match these labels to the members of the struct. For this example, we imported the encoding/json (https://pkg.go.dev/encoding/json), io/ioutil (https://pkg.go.dev/io/ioutil), net/http (https://pkg.go.dev/net/http) and strings (https://pkg.go.dev/strings) packages.

The toursFromJson() function is a custom function used to decode the body content in the JSON format of the HTTP response. It takes one argument, which is the JSON-formatted string fetched from the website. The function will return these values as structured data, specifically a slice containing instances of that tour object.

Within the toursFromJson() function, the first step is to create a slice tour of tour objects. The tour slice is initially set to size zero and an initial capacity of 20. Note that 20 is just a guess and not the exact number of objects that might be fetched. As slices can resize dynamically, you don't have to give a large initial capacity. The NewDecoder() built-in function returns a decoder that will read from the reader object passed to it. The NewReader() returns a reader that reads from the string passed to it. The Token() function returns the next JSON token in the input stream.

To transform the JSON-formatted text into the slice of tour objects, you declare a variable named tours and set its type to Tour. Next, a while-style for loop is used; the decoder.More() function reports whether or not any other elements are present in the current array or any other object is getting parsed. Within the for loop, the Decode() function of the decoder object reads the next JSON-encoded value from its input and stores it in the value pointed to by the argument passed to it. You pass the memory address of the tour object. Then you add the tour object to the tours slice using the append() function. In the end, the tours object is returned from the function.

Listing 2-58. Basic Program Illustrating How to Handle JSON Data in Go

```go
package main

import (
        "encoding/json"
        "fmt"
        "io/ioutil"
        "net/http"
        "strings"
)

const url = "http://services.explorecalifornia.org/json/
             tours.php"

func main() {
        resp, err := http.Get(url)

        if err != nil {
                panic(err)
        }
        fmt.Printf("Response Type: %T\n", resp)

        defer resp.Body.Close()

        bytes, err := ioutil.ReadAll(resp.Body)
        if err != nil {
                panic(err)
        }
        content := string(bytes)

        tours := toursFromJson(content)
```

```go
        for _, tour := range tours {
                fmt.Println(tour.Name, "  ", tour.Price)
        }
}

func toursFromJson(content string) []Tour {
        tours := make([]Tour, 0, 20) //slice of Tour array
                                      with initial size 0 and
                                      capacity 20

        decoder := json.NewDecoder(strings.NewReader(content))
        _, err := decoder.Token()
        if err != nil {
                panic(err)
        }

        var tour Tour
        for decoder.More() {
                err := decoder.Decode(&tour)
                if err != nil {
                        panic(err)
                }
                tours = append(tours, tour)
        }
        return tours
}

type Tour struct {
        Name, Price string
}
```

/*Output:

```
2 Days Adrift the Salton Sea     350
A Week of Wine      850
Amgen Tour of California Special      6000
Avila Beach Hot springs      1000
Big Sur Retreat      750
Channel Islands Excursion      150
Coastal Experience      1500
Cycle California: My Way      1200
Day Spa Package      550
Endangered Species Expedition      600
Fossil Tour      500
Hot Salsa Tour      400
Huntington Library and Pasadena Retreat Tour      225
In the Steps of John Muir      600
Joshua Tree: Best of the West Tour      150
Kids L.A. Tour      200
Mammoth Mountain Adventure      800
Matilija Hot springs      1000
Mojave to Malibu      200
Monterey to Santa Barbara Tour      2500
Mountain High Lift-off      800
Olive Garden Tour      75
Oranges & Apples Tour      350
Restoration Package      900
The Death Valley Survivor's Trek      250
The Mt. Whitney Climbers Tour      650
*/
```

Summary

This chapter covered the basic programming fundamentals you need to get started programming in Go, ranging from how to install the Go compiler and different IDEs available, the program structure of Go, to programming concepts. You also gained insight into how to use different data structures and programming features like variables, taking user input, available math operators and packages, managing memory and referencing values, and using pointers. You learned how to manage ordered values using arrays and slices, how to use maps to store key-value pairs, and how to define user-defined types using structs.

Managing program flow is a key point in programming, and this chapter also provided guidance into how to control the flow using different conditional statements, like `if`, `if..else`, `switch`, and `goto`. You also learned about the only type of loop available in Go that can be used in whichever way possible to achieve desired results.

Functions are an important part of modular programming. This chapter also covered how to use user-defined functions and attach methods to slices in Go. Another important capability of any program is the ability to read and write to files. This chapter also provided details into doing this. It also covered how to use HTTP package and handle JSON data. This is important to help programmers build applications that can effectively communicate with different web applications and services.

In the upcoming chapters, you'll go through Go recipes based on real-life scenarios in order to get a better understanding of the concepts covered in this chapter.

CHAPTER 3

Go Recipes: Programming Fundamentals and Basics

Go is a great language. It's compact, performant, and has great support for concurrency. This chapter covers common programming tasks and shows recipes for completing them. It covers language basics, date/time types, how to work with text files effectively, how to work with structs, and how to handle concurrency.

Numbers and Slices in Go

Listing 3-1 illustrates a Go recipe for calculating the mean of some numbers. The mean is defined as the sum of the numbers divided by the total numbers. The formula for calculating mean is as follows:

$$mean = \frac{\text{sum}\left(\text{numbers}\right)}{\text{total numbers}}$$

© Rumeel Hussain and Maryam Zulfiqar 2022
R. Hussain and M. Zulfiqar, *Beginning Go Programming*,
https://doi.org/10.1007/978-1-4842-8858-0_3

Listing 3-1. Go Recipe for Calculating Mean

```go
package main

import (
        "fmt"
)

func main() {
        ffmt.Println("Mean of {1,2,3} is: ", mean([]int
        {1, 2, 3}))          //mean=2
        fmt.Println("Mean of {1,2,3,4,5} is: ", mean([]int
        {1, 2, 3, 4, 5}))  //mean=3
}

func mean(nums []int) float64 {
        s := sum(nums)
        return (float64(s) / float64(len(nums)))
}

func sum(nums []int) int {
        total := 0
        for _, n := range nums {
                total += n
        }
        return total
}
```

Output:

```
Mean of {1,2,3} is:   2
Mean of {1,2,3,4,5} is:   3
```

Let's look at another example, where we need to write a function to calculate the median of a slice of type float32. The median is calculated by first sorting the values in numerical order. If the total count of items is odd, the middle value is the median. If the count is even, the average of the two middle items is considered the median. Listing 3-2 illustrates this concept.

Listing 3-2. Go Recipe for Calculating the Median

```go
package main

import (
        "fmt"
        "sort"
)

func main() {
        fmt.Println("Median of {56, 85, 92} is: ", median([]
        float64{56, 85, 92}))           //median= 85
        fmt.Println("Median of {56, 85, 92, 99} is: ", median([]
        float64{56, 85, 92, 99}))     //median= 88.5
}

func median(nums []float64) float64 {
        // Pass by Value: work on a copy, don't change the
        input slice
        vals := make([]float64, len(nums))
        copy(vals, nums)
        sort.Float64s(vals)

        i := len(vals) / 2
        if len(vals)%2 == 1 { //in case the slice has odd
                              number of items
                return vals[i]
        }
```

```
        //in case the slice has even number of items
        return (vals[i-1] + vals[i]) / 2
}
```

Output:

```
Median of {56, 85, 92} is:  85
Median of {56, 85, 92, 99} is:  88.5
```

Working with Maps in Go

In this section, we write a program to count how many times a word appears in the text. This is known as word frequency and is a common task in text processing. For example, in the sentence "to be or not to be," the frequency of "to" is 2, "be" is 2, "not" is 1, and "or" is 1. For this task, we use maps to store words and the word's count as the key-value pairs. Go maps don't generate panic when you try to access a nonexistent key. They instead return a zero value for the nonexistent key. In this example, the map values are integers and the zero value means the word count is zero. Listing 3-3 illustrates the recipe for accomplishing this.

Listing 3-3. Go Recipe for Working with Maps

```go
package main

import (
        "fmt"
)

var moby = []string{
        "shall", "pass", "shall", "away", "too"}

func main() {
        fmt.Println(frequency(moby))
}
```

```go
func frequency(words []string) map[string]int {
        freq := make(map[string]int)
        for _, w := range words {
                freq[w]++
        }
        return freq
}
```

Output:

```
map[away:1 pass:1 shall:2 too:1]
```

Go's Catch of Error Handling

In Go, errors are transmitted as an explicitly mentioned separate return value. The error-handling mechanism of Go is designed to make it easy for programs to infer error-returning functions. It is also designed to handle errors using the same language constructs that are used with tasks where no errors occur.

All errors in Go are of the type error, which has a built-in interface for error handling. By convention and as a common practice in Go, errors are usually the last value returned by a function. However, by using the errors.New() function, you can construct a custom error value with an associated error message given as input to the function. Furthermore, a nil value indicates that no error has occurred. Using the Error() method means you can use custom types as errors.

In the Go recipe shown in Listing 3-4, we illustrate how to use a custom type to raise an error that represents "argument error," which is basically an integer value that is not acceptable as input to a function. In this recipe, we use the &argError syntax to construct a new struct of type argError, which is a custom time. The &argError is passed two arguments to initialize the member fields—argument and problem. Furthermore, in the main() function, two loops are used to test the functioning of our custom error-returning functions. Remember that it is a good and common practice to use inline error checking on the if statement in Go.

Additionally, to programmatically utilize a custom error's data, you have to get the error as an instance of the custom error type through type assertion. The ok idiom in Go is used to test whether the key-value pair is present.

Listing 3-4. Go Recipe for Illustrating Error Handling

```go
package main

import (
        "errors"
        "fmt"
)

func function1(argument int) (int, error) {
        if argument == 12 {
                return -1, errors.New("12 is not an acceptable
                argument")
        }

        return argument + 3, nil
}

type argError struct {
        argument int
        problem  string
}
```

```go
func (e *argError) Error() string {
        return fmt.Sprintf("%d - %s", e.argument, e.problem)
}

func function2(argument int) (int, error) {
        if argument == 12 {

                return -1, &argError{argument, "Unacceptable
                Argument"}
        }
        return argument + 3, nil
}

func main() {

        for _, i := range []int{7, 12} {
                if r, e := function1(i); e != nil {
                        fmt.Println("function1 Failed to Execute
                        Successfully \nError:", e)
                } else {
                        fmt.Println("function1 Executed
                        Successfully:", r)
                }
        }
        for _, i := range []int{70, 12} {
                if r, e := function2(i); e != nil {
                        fmt.Println("function2 Failed to
                        Execute Successfully \nError:", e)
                } else {
                        fmt.Println("function1 Executed
                        Successfully:", r)
                }
        }
```

```
    _, e := function2(42)
    if ae, ok := e.(*argError); ok {
            fmt.Println(ae.argument)
            fmt.Println(ae.problem)
    }
}
```

/*Output:

```
function1 Executed Successfully: 10
function1 Failed to Execute Successfully
Error: 12 is not an acceptable argument
function1 Executed Successfully: 73
function2 Failed to Execute Successfully
Error: 12 - Unacceptable Argument
*/
```

Defer and Panic Recovery

You'll sometimes use resources that need to be released once you are finished using them. One of the more important resources in programming is memory. Memory is managed automatically by the garbage collectors. However, there are other resources, such as files, that need to be explicitly closed.

There is usually a limit in the operating system to how many open files a process can have. If this limit is reached, maybe because your server has been running for a couple of days, the server will start showing different errors. In Go, the built-in keyword defer is designed exactly for these cases.

In Go, the defer keyword makes sure that a function call is delayed and executed sometime later, during the execution of a program. It is also used for cleanup purposes. The defer keyword, as compared to other programming languages, is similar to the ensure and finally keywords.

In the Go recipe shown in Listing 3-5, we use the `defer` keyword by creating a file and writing data to it. For this purpose, we create a file, write data in it, and finally close the file when the required task is completed. Notice that we do not close the file immediately after getting the file object using `createFile()`. Rather, the `defer` keyword delays the closing of the file. In Go, the `closeFile()` function is used to close an open file. The deferred commands are executed at the end of the enclosing function. In this case, the execution of the deferred function will occur after `main()` and `writeFile()` have finished their execution. Remember that, even with a deferred function, it is important to check for any errors when closing a file.

Listing 3-5. Go Recipe for Defer and Panic Recovery

```go
package main

import (
        "fmt"
        "os"
)

func main() {

        f := createFile("defer-eg.txt")
        defer closeFile(f)
        writeFile(f)
}

func createFile(fileName string) *os.File {
        fmt.Println("Creating File with name ", fileName)
        file, err := os.Create(fileName)
        if err != nil {
                panic(err)
        }
```

```go
        return file
}

func writeFile(fileName *os.File) {
        fmt.Println("Writing Data to File with name ",
        fileName.Name())
        fmt.Fprintln(fileName, "Hi, My name is Maryam.")

}

func closeFile(file *os.File) {
        fmt.Println("Closing File with name ", file.Name())
        err := file.Close()

        if err != nil {
                fmt.Fprintf(os.Stderr, "Error: %v\n", err)
                os.Exit(1)
        }
}
```

Output:

```
Creating File with name  defer-eg.txt
Writing Data to File with name  defer-eg.txt
Closing File with name  defer-eg.txt
```

In Go, the panic idiom is used to return errors. However, in some cases, the Go program can panic, which is similar to an exception, and sometimes it's likely to guard against these panics. A *panic* usually refers to something that went wrong unexpectedly. It is normally used for failing fast on errors that aren't raised during the normal execution of the program, or for errors that cannot be managed in a graceful manner.

Throughout the recipes in this book, we illustrate the use of panic to ensure the behavior of our Go programs against any unexpected error(s). Aborting a program is one of the most common use cases of panic. For example, a program can be aborted if a function returns an error that you either have no clue how to handle or don't want to handle.

The Go recipe shown in Listing 3-6 illustrates how to use panic when an unexpected error occurs while you're creating a new file. Running this Go recipe will cause the application to panic. It will also print a message indicating the error along with related goroutine traces for the user. Furthermore, the application will exit with a status not equal to zero. When the first line of the main function runs, the panic gets triggered. In this case, the program will exit without executing the rest of the code. Note that, unlike other programming languages that use exceptions to perform error handling wherever possible, Go uses error-indicating return values to obtain the same results.

Listing 3-6. Go Recipe for Using Panic with Unexpected Errors

```go
package main

import "os"

func main() {

        //Trigger panic with Custom Error Message
        panic("Problem!")

        _, err := os.Create("/tmp/file")

        if err != nil {
                panic(err)
        }
}
```

Output:

```
panic: Problem!

goroutine 1 [running]:
main.main()
        ../.../code-3.6.go:8 +0x27
exit status 2
```

Hands-on Challenge

Suppose you have to write a function called `filter`. The function must take two arguments as input. The first argument is a predicate function named `isOdd` and the second is a slice of `int` type containing eight non-negative integers. In general, a statement that can be true or false is referred to as a *predicate*. Predicates in programming refer to functions that take a single argument as input and return a `bool` value as output. The `isOdd` function should take an integer as an input argument and return `true` if the number is odd and `false` otherwise. The `filter` function must return from the passed slice the values that the predicate function returns `true` for. The output of the program should be odd numbers from the passed input slice.

Solution

Listing 3-7 illustrates one of the possible solutions for this hands-on challenge.

Listing 3-7. Solution for the Hands-on Challenge

```go
package main

import (
        "fmt"
)

func main() {
        values := []int{22, 85, 36, 94, 50, 67, 17, 18}
        fmt.Println("Before Filtering: ", values)
        fmt.Println("After Filtering: ", filter(isOdd, values))
}

//filter returns a slice with only the values that pred(val)
returned true
func filter(pred func(int) bool, values []int) []int {
        var out []int
        for _, val := range values {
                if pred(val) {
                        out = append(out, val)
                }
        }
        return out
}

func isOdd(n int) bool {
        return n%2 == 1
}

    /*Output:

[85 67 17]
*/
```

Summary

This chapter provided recipes that illustrate the programming fundamentals of the Go language. Working through these recipes provides you with hands-on experience with Go. The recipes covered in this chapter include basic Go programs, like calculating the mean and the median, that help you understand maps, slices, and arrays in a more efficient manner. These recipes also covered how error handling is performed in Go and the use of defer and panic recovery.

In the upcoming chapter, we provide recipes for working with text in Go.

CHAPTER 4

Working with Text

Real-world applications work with a lot of textual data. Unlike languages like C++ and Java, in Go, strings behave as read-only slices of bytes. Furthermore, Unicode text using UTF-8 encoding is used to represent bytes of strings. Several Go libraries are available for the purpose of string manipulation, for example, packages like `strings`, `unicode`, and `regexp`. Note that, in Go, strings are *immutable* or read-only, meaning that their value cannot be changed after their creation. Trying to make changes to them will raise errors. This chapter discusses how to work with text in the Go language. Specifically, it covers string formatting, Unicode data handling, and using regular expressions in the Go language.

Go String Formatting and Working with Unicode

Computers were initially developed for countries like the United Kingdom and the United States of America, which are English-speaking. At that time, the capacity of a single byte was up to 255 numbers, which was enough to represent the English alphabet set using the ASCII format. However, the need to encode letters in more than one byte emerged when other countries started using computers. Hence, Unicode was developed. In Unicode, characters or code points are encoded to specific numbers. These numbers are, in turn, encoded into bytes as per the encoding scheme. For example, UTF-8 is used for encoding code strings. In Go,

© Rumeel Hussain and Maryam Zulfiqar 2022
R. Hussain and M. Zulfiqar, *Beginning Go Programming*,
https://doi.org/10.1007/978-1-4842-8858-0_4

Unicode code points are referred to as *runes*. Additionally, Unicode is designed to be a superset of the ASCII format. Furthermore, Unicode is designed to include all characters present in the world's writing systems, inclusive of several diacritical marks, different accents, and control codes such as carriage returns, tabs, and so on.

The Go recipe shown in Listing 4-1 illustrates a function that returns the total count of characters present in a given sentence. The given input can also contain Unicode formatted characters. A sentence is passed as an input argument to the lineLength() function. The input is basically a slice of strings named word. You must calculate the length of the word in terms of characters. Remember that this is different from calculating length in terms of bytes. If the built-in function of len() is used, it will return the length in bytes. On the other hand, if you use the RuneCountInString() function from the unicode/utf package, it gives you the total number of runes in a string. Since the for loop will only iterate each word, to keep a record of the number of spaces, you can use the formula (length of the word)-1. At the function's end, you return the sum of the total and the number of spaces. Note that the angular brackets in the string passed as input are Unicode-encoded.

Listing 4-1. Go Recipe for String Formatting and Working with Unicode

```
package main

import (
        "fmt"
        "unicode/utf8"
)

func lineLength(words []string) int {
        total := 0
        for _, word := range words {
```

```
                total += utf8.RuneCountInString(word)
        }
        numSpaces := len(words) - 1
        return total + numSpaces
}

func main() {
        words := []string{"«", "Don't", "Panic", "»"}
        //UTF-8 angular brackets
        fmt.Println("Length: ", lineLength(words))
}
```

Output:

Length: 15

Case-Insensitive Comparisons in Go

In Go, strings are UTF-8 encoded. The strings package of Go provides an EqualFold method for performing case-insensitive comparisons of two strings.

The example in Listing 4-2 demonstrates a function that returns the English name for a Greek letter. In English, there are upper- and lowercase letters. Generally, to run a case-insensitive comparison of strings, you have to convert the letters in a string to either one of the cases for performing the comparison. However, this is not the case with every language. For example, in Greek, the letter sigma has three forms (Σ, σ, and ς). Here, the string.toUpper() function won't work. Rather, the string.EqualFold() function would be handy.

Listing 4-2 defines struct letters with member fields Symbol to store Greek symbols and the English field to store the associated English name. The letters slice will hold the symbols and names for you. If the letter passed is not found, the program will return an error message. Note that since **Σ, σ,** and **ς** are all forms of sigma, the code will print "Sigma" for each of these letters.

Listing 4-2. Go Recipe to Illustrate Case-Sensitive Comparisons

```go
package main

import (
        "fmt"
        "strings"
)

type Letter struct {
        Symbol, English string
}

var letters = []Letter{
        {"Σ", "Sigma"},
}

func englishFor(greek string) (string, error) {
        for _, letter := range letters {
                if strings.EqualFold(greek, letter.Symbol) {
                        return letter.English, nil
                }
        }
        return "", fmt.Errorf("Unknown Greek Letter: %#v", greek)
}
func main() {
        fmt.Println(englishFor("Σ"))
        fmt.Println(englishFor("σ"))
        fmt.Println(englishFor("ς"))
        fmt.Println(englishFor("�"))
}
```

/*Output:

```
Sigma <nil>
Sigma <nil>
Sigma <nil>
 Unknown Greek Letter: "�"
*/
```

Regular Expressions and Reading Text Files with Go

Go includes built-in support for in the form of the regexp package. The recipe in Listing 4-3 demonstrates some of the common use cases for the regexp package in Go. In this code, on line#12, the regexp.MatchString() function checks directly whether the regular expression and string match. The regexp.MatchString() function returns true or false after checking. On line#17, the Compile() function is used to generate a regex object that can be used to match text instead of specifying regular expressions directly. As shown on line#58, the MustCompile() version of Compile() should be used instead. This is because, instead of returning an error, the MustCompile() version will cause panic, which is a much safer practice to use with global variables.

Lines 21 to 48 illustrate the various built-in functions to find matches, submatches, start and end indexes of matches or submatches, and so on, using a regular expression and string passed as an argument. You can also limit the number of returned matches by passing a non-negative integer as an argument, as shown on line#53. The ReplaceAllString() function, as shown on line#64, can be used to replace a subset of strings with the desired value. For more information on the regex package, refer to the official documentation (https://pkg.go.dev/regexp).

Listing 4-3. Go Recipe for Using Regular Expressions

```go
package main

import (
        "bytes"
        "fmt"
        "regexp"
)

func main() {
        /* Checking directly if the regex pattern matches a
        string */
        match, _ := regexp.MatchString("p([a-z]+)ch", "preach")
        fmt.Println(match)

        /* Compiling an Optimized Regexp struct to get a
           Regexp object that can be used to match against text */
        r, _ := regexp.Compile("p([a-z]+)ch")

        /* MatchString checks if passed string has any match of
           the regular expression */
        fmt.Println(r.MatchString("preach"))

        /* FindString checks if the passed string holds any text
           matching leftmost text of the regular expression */
        fmt.Println(r.FindString("preach patch"))

        /* FindStringIndex finds the first match in the passed
           string that matches the regular expression and returns
           the start and end indexes of match instead text */
        fmt.Println("Start and End Indexes of Match:",
                r.FindStringIndex("pinch pouch"))
```

```
/* FindStringSubmatch finds the leftmost match in the
   passed string that matches the regular expression
   and the submatch */
fmt.Println(r.FindStringSubmatch("poach pitch"))

/* FindStringSubmatch finds the leftmost match in the
   passed string that matches the regular expression
   and the submatch and returns the start and end index
   instead of text. Here, the end index for match is
   exclusive. */
fmt.Println(r.FindStringSubmatchIndex("punch"))

/*The All variants finds all matches in passed string*/
/* Find all matches in a given input for a regular
expression*/
fmt.Println(r.FindAllString("parch patch pitch", -1))

/* FindAllStringSubmatchIndex returns a slice containing
   all of the matches regular of the expression*/
fmt.Println("Indexes of All Matches and Submatches:",
r.FindAllStringSubmatchIndex(
         "potch pooch porch", -1))

/* Limiting the number of returned matches by passing a
   non-negative integer as an argument */
fmt.Println(r.FindAllString("prelaunch postlaunch
pitch", 2))

/* Checking if the byte slice contains text matching to
   regular expression*/
fmt.Println(r.Match([]byte("pinch")))
```

```
/* Using MustCompile with global variables*/
r = regexp.MustCompile("p([a-z]+)ch")
fmt.Println("regexp:", r)

/* Replacing string subsets with other values */
fmt.Println(r.ReplaceAllString("pinch it!", "hurt"))

/* Transforming matched text with a specified function.*/
in := []byte("The prelaunch")
out := r.ReplaceAllFunc(in, bytes.ToUpper)
fmt.Println(string(out))
}
```

/**Output:

```
true
true
preach
Start and End Indexes of Match: [0 5]
[poach oa]
[0 5 1 3]
[parch patch pitch]
Indexes of All Matches and Submatches: [[0 5 1 3] [6 11 7 9]
[12 17 13 15]]
[prelaunch postlaunch]
true
regexp: p([a-z]+)ch
hurt it!
The PRELAUNCH
*/
```

Let's suppose you have a ledger of stocks saved on your system in a text format. There are 12 shares of Microsoft for $234.57 and 10 shares of Tesla of $692.40. Suppose that, after automatically parsing the ledger, the text must be transferred into a slice of struct type `transaction`.

To do this, first write a function that will be used for parsing one line of the ledger at a time. Additionally, the ledger is not in a structured format, such as YAML,CSV, XML, or JSON. Because of this, it is necessary to use regular expressions to perform parsing. In Go, the `regexp` package provides several regular expressions that programmers can use. To learn about the syntax for using regular expressions, refer to the `regexp/syntax` package's official documentation (`https://pkg.go.dev/regexp/syntax`).

Listing 4-4 is one sample solution to solving this scenario. In Listing 4-4, you must first define the regular expression to parse a single line. Remember that it is considered good practice to always give an example of your regular expressions in the form of comments code for better understanding. Here, the `MustCompile()` function will cause panic if the regular expression is not valid.

Note that this program declared the variable holding the regular expression at the global level so that it is accessible by the entire program and the panic will cause the entire program to crash. In the regular expression, `\d+` is a placeholder for numbers. The `+` sign means one or more characters are allowed. The expression `([A-Z]+)` means that uppercase characters are acceptable. The `\$` is for a dollar sign. The expression `(\d+(\.\d+)?)` is used for printing prices. It accepts one or more numbers after the dollar sign followed by a (`.`) and then one or more numbers. Thus you have declared the `Transaction` struct.

The `parseLine()` function takes a string as an input argument and returns an object of `Transaction` type along with an error. Within the function, we first check whether the string passed matches the regular expression using the `FindStringSubmatch()` function. It returns a slice of matches. If there are no matches, it returns an error and an empty transaction object. When there's a match, it assigns the values to the

respective member fields of the transaction type object trans. Since
regular expressions deal with text, the matches are going to be strings. You
need to convert them to integers in the case of the volume and to floats
in the case of the price. You can do this by using the strconv.Atoi()
and strconv.ParseFloat() functions, respectively. While doing so, you
can ignore the returned errors, because you know the regular expression
matches a valid string that can be converted safely into a number.

Listing 4-4. Go Recipe for Reading and Parsing Text Files

```go
package main

import (
        "fmt"
        "log"
        "regexp"
        "strconv"
)

/*
12 shares of MSFT for $234.57
10 shares of TSLA for $692.4
*/

var transRe = regexp.MustCompile(`(\d+) shares of ([A-Z]+) for
                \$(\d+(\.\d+)?)`)

type Transaction struct {
        Symbol string
        Volume int
        Price  float64
}
```

```go
func parseLine(line string) (Transaction, error) {
        matches := transRe.FindStringSubmatch(line)
        if matches == nil {
                return Transaction{}, fmt.Errorf("Bad Line:
                %q", line)
        }
        var trans Transaction
        trans.Symbol = matches[2]
        trans.Volume, _ = strconv.Atoi(matches[1])
        trans.Price, _ = strconv.ParseFloat(matches[3], 64)
        return trans, nil
}

func main() {
        line := "12 shares of MSFT for $234.57"
        t, err := parseLine(line)
        if err != nil {
                log.Fatal(err)
        }
        fmt.Printf("%+v\n", t)
}

/*\Output:

{Symbol:MSFT Volume:12 Price:234.57}
*/
```

Suppose you are running a Linux machine and would like to know how many times your system has rebooted. This information can be obtained from a sys.log file. Using the grep utility, you can search this file for the sentence "System is rebooting". In the following example, you will write a function that will work like the grep utility and show lines that contain the terms you are searching for.

As shown in Listing 4-5, the grep() function takes two inputs—an io. Reader object from which the text will be read and the term you have to search for. Additionally, it returns a slice of strings matching the desired term. The NewScanner() returns a new scanner to read from the io. Reader. The strings.Contain() determines whether the current text contains the required terms. If it does, you append the current line to the matches slice. You need to check if there was an error while scanning. If not, you return the matches.

Listing 4-5. Go Recipe for Writing a Function Similar to the grep Utility

```go
package main

import (
        "bufio"
        "fmt"
        "io"
        "log"
        "strings"
)

func main() {
        r := strings.NewReader("This is a sample code. Learn to
        code properly")
        term := "code"
        matches, err := (grep(r, term))
        if err != nil {
                log.Fatalln(err.Error())
        }
        if matches != nil {
                fmt.Println("Lines containing \"", term,
                "\" are :")
                fmt.Println(matches)
```

```
        } else {
                fmt.Println("Query term is not present")
        }
}

//grep returns lines in r that contain term
func grep(r io.Reader, term string) ([]string, error) {
        var matches []string
        s := bufio.NewScanner(r)
        for s.Scan() {
                if strings.Contains(s.Text(), term) {
                        matches = append(matches, s.Text())
                }
        }
        if err := s.Err(); err != nil {
                return nil, err
        }
        return matches, nil
}
```

Output:

```
Lines containing " code " are :
[This is a sample code. Learn to code properly]
```

Hands-on Challenge

Write a Go program to return the count of occurrences of Go subcommands from a given file. The file contains text in the following format.

```
1542784314:0;git push
1542784378:0;ls
1542784308:0;go test
1542784310:0;go test -v
```

Solution

Listing 4-6 shows one possible solution to this hands-on challenge.

Listing 4-6. Go Recipe Showing One Solution to the Hands-on Challenge

```go
package main

import (
        "bufio"
        "fmt"
        "os"
        "regexp"
)

/* Example data in file to read
1542784314:0;git push
1542784378:0;ls
1542784308:0;go test
1542784310:0;go run -v
1542784311:0;go test -v
*/

var cmdRe = regexp.MustCompile(`;go ([a-z]+)`)

//cmdFreq returns the frequency of the go subcommand from the
given file
func cmdFreq(fileName string) (map[string]int, error) {
        file, err := os.Open(fileName)
        if err != nil {
                return nil, err
        }
        defer file.Close()
```

```go
        freqs := make(map[string]int)
        s := bufio.NewScanner(file)
        for s.Scan() {
                matches := cmdRe.FindStringSubmatch(s.Text())
                if len(matches) == 0 {
                        continue
                }
                cmd := matches[1]
                freqs[cmd]++
        }
        if err := s.Err(); err != nil {
                return nil, err
        }
        return freqs, nil
}

func main() {
        result, _ := cmdFreq("./sample.txt")
        for key, _ := range result {
                fmt.Println("Subcommand: ", key, " Count: ",
                result[key])
        }
}

/*Output:

Subcommand:  test  Count:  2
Subcommand:  run  Count:  1
*/
```

Summary

This chapter included Go recipes based on different scenarios to provide hands-on experience to users on advance topics like string formatting, reading text files, performing case-sensitive comparisons, and using regular expressions.

Being able to define data types is critical, so in the next chapter, we provide recipes on structs, methods, and interfaces.

CHAPTER 5

Structs, Methods, and Interfaces

Go supports structs (short for *structures*) that allow programmers to define user-defined types. Related data that exhibits a "has-a" relationship can be grouped into a single logical unit using structs. Methods in Go are functions that can be tied to user-defined types to define their behavior. Another important feature of the Go language is the concept of interfaces. In Go, structs and interfaces go hand in hand to organize methods and data handling. An interface can be defined as a collection of method signatures that can be implemented by any other type. Implementing an interface in Go merely means implementing the methods defined by that interface. Furthermore, an interface only defines but does not declare the behavior of an object. To simplify, a *struct* defines the fields of an object, e.g., a shape's type and color, whereas an *interface* defines the methods that can be used with that object, e.g., setting and returning a shape's color. This chapter provides Go recipes related to the usage of structs, methods, and interfaces.

Go Structs, Methods, and Interfaces

In this section, we provide recipes to illustrate how to define user-defined data types using structs, define methods associated with structs, and use interfaces having a collection of methods to associate with structs. We use

© Rumeel Hussain and Maryam Zulfiqar 2022
R. Hussain and M. Zulfiqar, *Beginning Go Programming*,
https://doi.org/10.1007/978-1-4842-8858-0_5

an example of a home automation system that uses sensors to send events details to a server, e.g., a door or a thermostat sending events.

Structs

In Go, whenever there is a need to define user-defined data types, `structs` are used. They allow programmers to group together logically related data. For example, a struct named `Person` can be used to group related information like first name, last name, age, and so on, in order to create a data record. In other words, structs can be used to store collections of items. Structs can be used to group user-defined data types as well as Go's built-in data types. They also improve the modularity of your code and help create and pass around complex data structures.

Declaring Structs in Go

Listing 5-1 illustrates the declaration of a struct in Go. The declaration starts with the `type` keyword, followed by the user-defined name for the structure. This can be anything of your choice, and in the end, the `struct` keyword indicates that a new struct is being declared. Within the curly brackets, you can specify any number of data fields that you want to group. For each data field, it is important to specify the name and the data type.

Listing 5-1. General Format for Declaring Structs in Go

```
type identifier struct{
  field1 data_type
  field2 data_type
  field3 data_type
}
```

While naming a struct, always remember that neither the struct nor its fields are exported to other packages if the identifiers of the struct and its fields start with lowercase letters. In Go, to export the identifiers, i.e., to allow accessibility to other packages, it is necessary to make ensure that the name begins with an uppercase letter.

Creating Instances of a Struct Type

There are multiple ways to instantiate new instances of a struct type. Consider Listing 5-2, where a circle struct is declared with three data fields—length, breadth, and color. Line#15 depicts how to use a struct without explicitly instantiating a new instance of that struct type. The var keyword initializes a variable circle1 of the type circle. The dot notation (.) assigns values to the fields of the struct instance, as illustrated on line#19. Line#26 depicts how to create a struct instance using a struct literal, and you can skip values for data fields in this way. Lines 32 and 39 use the new keyword to instantiate new instances of the circle struct. The difference between circle3 and circle4 is that circle3 is a pointer to an instance of circle, whereas circle4 is an instance of circle. Similarly, you can instantiate a new instance of the struct type using the pointer address operator (&), as shown in lines 46, 49, and 54.

Listing 5-2. Go Recipe for Creating Instances of a Struct Type

```go
package main

import (
        "fmt"
)

type circle struct {
        length  float32
        breadth float32
        color   string
}
```

```go
func main() {
        //use struct without instantiating a new instance
        fmt.Println("Without Instantiating: ", circle{10.5,
        25.10, "red"})

        //Creating Instance of Struct type
        var circle1 circle
        circle1.length = 20 //dot notation to assign values
        circle1.breadth = 30
        circle1.color = "Yellow"
        fmt.Println("Circle1: ", circle1)

        //Creating a Struct Instance Using a Struct Literal
        var circle2 = circle{length: 10, color: "Green"}
        /* breadth
        value is skipped */
        fmt.Println("Circle2: ", circle2)

        //Struct Instantiation Using new Keyword
        circle3 := new(circle) /* circle3 is a pointer to an
        instance of circle */
        circle3.length = 10
        circle3.breadth = 20
        circle3.color = "Red"
        fmt.Println("Circle3: ", circle3)

        var circle4 = new(circle) //circle4 is an instance
        of circle
        circle4.length = 40
        circle4.color = "Blue"
        fmt.Println("Circle4: ", circle4)
```

```go
//Struct Instantiation Using Pointer Address Operator
var circle5 = &circle{10, 20, "Green"} //Can't skip
any value!
fmt.Println(circle5)

var circle6 = &circle{}
circle6.length = 10
circle6.color = "Red"
fmt.Println(circle6) //value for breadth is skipped

var circle7 = &circle{}
(*circle7).breadth = 10
(*circle7).color = "Blue"
fmt.Println(circle7) //value for length is skipped
}
```

Output:

```
Without Instantiating:  {10.5 25.1 red}
Circle1:  {20 30 Yellow}
Circle2:  {10 0 Green}
Circle3:  &{10 20 Red}
Circle4:  &{40 0 Blue}
Circle5:  &{10 20 Green}
Circle6:  &{10 0 Red}
Circle7:  &{0 10 Blue}
```

Recipe to See Structs in Action

Listing 5-3 illustrates the use of structs through an example of a house automation system that uses sensors that send different event details. Because there can be multiple different sensors, to store the information of different events generated by them, you first define a struct named event. The member fields of the event struct are used to identify the instrument that generated the event (in this case, a door or thermostat) and the time that the event has occurred.

It also defines instrument-specific events, namely DoorEvent and TemperatureEvent, to illustrate the concept of *type embedding* in Go. Type embedding is a technique where you include one type into another but as a parameter without a name. Through type embedding, all of the exported parameters and methods defined on the embedded type are also accessible to the type within which the type is embedded. Both the DoorEvent and TemperatureEvent structs embed the Event type. In addition to the member fields of the Event struct, each struct also has its own respective member fields as well. The NewDoorEvent() function takes input parameters that will be used to create an object of the struct DoorEvent. Upon entering the function, you perform some validation to make sure that the ID is not empty. Next, you create an evt variable of the embedded type Event. At the end of the function, you return the pointer to the evt variable containing the event details. If you're familiar with C or C++, it might seem odd to return a pointer to something that is allocated on the stack. The Go compiler performs an escape analysis and moves the event details being used outside of the function from the stack to the heap.

Listing 5-3. Go Recipe for Using Structs

```go
package main
import (
        "fmt"
        "log"
        "time"
)

type Event struct {
        ID    string
        Time time.Time
}
```

```go
type DoorEvent struct {
       Event
       Action string //open, close
}

type TemperatureEvent struct {
       Event
       Value float32
}

func NewDoorEvent(id string, time time.Time, action string)
(*DoorEvent, error) {
       if id == "" {
              return nil, fmt.Errorf("empty id")
       }

       evt := DoorEvent{
              Event:  Event{id, time},
              Action: action,
       }
       return &evt, nil
}

func main() {
       evt, err := NewDoorEvent("front door", time.
       Now(), "open")
       if err != nil {
              log.Fatal(err)
       }
       fmt.Printf("%+v\n", evt)
}
```

Output:

```
&{Event:{ID:front door Time:2022-02-14 17:45:54.9964674 +0500
PKT m=+0.003330501} Action:open}
```

Methods

Methods can be defined and attached to user-defined data types. Go methods and functions are similar to each other except that methods have an additional receiver argument. Methods use this receiver argument to access different properties associated with the receiver object. However, it is possible for the receiver to be a struct type or non-struct type. One important thing to remember is both the receiver and the receiver type used with a method should reside in the same package. Furthermore, if a receiver type is already defined in a different package, you cannot create a method for it. This includes the built-in types like string, float, int, and so on. Trying to do so will result in errors at compile time.

Declaring Methods in Go

The syntax for declaring a method in Go is shown in Listing 5-4. The func keyword is followed by a receiver name and its type, then the method name is followed by the list of input parameters, and finally the return type is shown, if the method returns anything.

Listing 5-4. General Format for Declaring Methods in Go

```
func(reciver_name Type) method_name(parameter_list)
(return_type){
// Code
}
```

Recipe to See Methods in Action

Look at the Go recipe in Listing 5-5, which illustrates the workings of a thermostat, which is a device used to control and measure temperature. First, you define a struct named thermostat. It has two member fields—ID, which is a string, and value of float32 type. Note that the ID field is exported (it's public), so its name starts with an uppercase letter. Since the value field is not exported, it's private, which is why its name starts with a lowercase letter. The Value() function gets a receiver key, which is a pointer type to the thermostat. It returns an internal value of type float32. The Set() function sets the value on the thermostat according to the value specified as its argument. Remember, pointer receivers are used with methods that change a struct. It is also possible for methods to have a type without any receiver. For example, the Kind() function in Listing 5-5 is one such method.

Listing 5-5. Go Recipe for Using Methods in Go

```go
package main

import (
        "fmt"
)

//A thermostat measures and controls the temperature
type Thermostat struct {
        ID    string
        value float64
}

//Value return the current temperature in Celsius
func (t *Thermostat) Value() float64 {
        return t.value
}
```

```go
//Set tells the thermostat to set the temperature
func (t *Thermostat) Set(value float64) {
        t.value = value
}

//Kind returns the device kind
func (t *Thermostat) Kind() string {
        return "thermostat"
}

func main() {
        t := Thermostat{"Living Room", 16.2}
        fmt.Printf("%s Before: %.2f\n", t.ID, t.Value())
        t.Set(18)
        fmt.Printf("%s After: %.2f\n", t.ID, t.Value())
}
```

/*Output:

```
Living Room Before: 16.20
Living Room After: 18.00
*/
```

Interfaces

Go is a multi-paradigm language, as it shares aspects of functional, imperative, and object-oriented programming. Even though it may seem that Go shares much from the OOP paradigm, there is an exception. Go does not support inheritance using classes; rather, it chooses composition over inheritance and uses structs and interfaces to achieve this goal.

Declaring Interfaces in Go

In Go, an *interface* is an abstract type, i.e., it is used to describe all the methods that can be implemented by a type. However, interfaces are limited to providing the method signatures and not their implementation. The implementation of the methods is entirely up to the type implementing the interface. Hence, it can be stated that interfaces only define, and do not declare, the behavior of an object of a specific type.

Listing 5-6 illustrates creating an interface in Go. First comes the type keyword, followed by the interface name, which can be the programmers' choice, except for the Go language reserved keywords. In the end is the interface keyword. The associated method signatures are enclosed within curly braces, as shown in Listing 5-6.

Listing 5-6. General Format for Declaring Interfaces in Go

```
type interface_name interface{

// Method signatures

}
```

Implementing Interfaces in Go

In Go, it is mandatory to implement all of the methods declared in an interface when implementing it. Furthermore, unlike other languages that require an implement keyword to implement interfaces, Go implements interfaces implicitly. Listing 5-7 illustrates how to declare and implement an interface in Go.

Listing 5-7. Go Recipe for Implementing Interfaces in Go

```go
package main

import (
        "fmt"
)

// Creating an Interface
type Shape interface {
        // Method Signatures
        Area() float64
        Perimeter() float64
}

type Rectangle struct {
        length   float64
        breadth float64
}

// Implementing Methods of the Shape Interface
func (r Rectangle) Area() float64 {
        return r.length * r.breadth
}

func (r Rectangle) Perimeter() float64 {
        return 2 * (r.length + r.breadth)
}

// Main Method
func main() {
        // Accessing Elements of the Shape Interface
        var s Shape
        s = Rectangle{10, 14}
```

```
        fmt.Println("Area of Shape :", s.Area())
        fmt.Println("Perimeter of Shape:", s.Perimeter())
}
```

/*Output:

```
Area of Shape : 140
Perimeter of Shape: 48
*/
```

Recipe to See Interfaces in Action

Let's look at a Go recipe to learn how to use interfaces. Suppose that you have several sensors and want to print them all. In this case, you first need to define a user-defined type, Sensor, which is used to store information regarding a sensor. Since all of the sensors need a similar functionality, you can use interfaces for this purpose.

Listing 5-8 illustrates the use of interfaces in Go. Here, you have a thermostat struct with three associated methods. The other struct is that of camera, which has the same methods as those associated with the thermostat. The printAll() function prints the ID of any sensor. You can use an interface for printing purposes. It gets a slice of sensors and, for every sensor, prints the ID and the kind. In main(), you create a slice of type Sensors that will contain the Thermostat and Camera structs and print their details.

Listing 5-8. Go Recipe for Using Interfaces in Go

```
package main

import (
        "fmt"
)
```

```go
//A thermostat measures and controls the temperature
type Thermostat struct {
        id     string
        value float64
}

//Value return the current temperature in Celsius
func (t *Thermostat) Value() float64 {
        return t.value
}

//ID returns the thermostat ID
func (t *Thermostat) ID() string {
        return t.id
}

//Set tells the thermostat to set the temperature
func (t *Thermostat) Set(value float64) {
        t.value = value
}

//Kind returns the device kind
func (t *Thermostat) Kind() string {
        return "thermostat"
}

//Camera is a security camera
type Camera struct {
        id string
}

//ID return the camera ID
func (c *Camera) ID() string {
        return c.id
}
```

```go
func (*Camera) Kind() string {
        return "camera"
}

type Sensor interface {
        ID() string
        Kind() string
}

func printAll(sensors []Sensor) {
        for _, s := range sensors {
                fmt.Printf("%s <%s>\n", s.ID(), s.Kind())
        }
}

func main() {
        t := Thermostat{"Living Room", 16.2}
        c := Camera{"Baby Room"}

        sensors := []Sensor{&t, &c}
        printAll(sensors)
        /*fmt.Printf("%s Before: %.2f\n", t.ID, t.Value())
        t.Set(18)
        fmt.Printf("%s After: %.2f\n", t.ID, t.Value())*/
}

   /*Output:

Living Room <thermostat>
Baby Room <camera>
*/
```

Empty Interface and Working with IOTA in Go

When an interface type does not specify any methods, it is called an empty interface. In Go, empty interfaces handle values of unknown type. An empty interface can also accommodate values of any type. Another concept to look into in Go is that of IOTA. IOTA is an identifier that is used with constants that use auto-increment numbers. In simple words, IOTA is essentially a counter that starts with zero and increments by 1. It can be used to create effective constants and enums in Go. In this section, we discuss the use of empty interfaces and IOTA in Go through examples.

JSON Encoding/Decoding

Go offers built-in support for JSON encoding and decoding, including to and from built-in and custom data types. The encoding/json package allows you to do encoding of JSON data as defined in the RFC 7159. When working with data, you usually want to encode some Go struct into a json string. Let's look at the JSON Marshall function, as defined in the official documentation (https://pkg.go.dev/encoding/json#Manual).

As shown in Figure 5-1, the Marshal() function gets an object of any type, which is an alias for an empty interface, i.e., interface{}, and returns a byte array containing the JSON encoding of the passed argument. The JSON Marshal() can marshal several types, such as integers, strings, time.Time, and so on. These types don't share common methods and hence the only interface that satisfies them all is the empty interface. The empty interface says nothing. It's a way to bypass the type system followed in Go. However, you should only use an empty interface as a last resort.

func Marshal

```
func Marshal(v any) ([]byte, error)
```

Figure 5-1. *Format of the Marshal function from a JSON package*

Let's look at an example to get a better understanding. In Listing 5-9, assume that you have several kinds of events, for example, ClickEvent and HoverEvent. There is also a counter for how many times each event is fired. The recordEvent() function records the counts. It gets an empty interface because these two events and any other event in the system do not have anything in common. In this function, you use the switch statement to check the type of the current event. If it's a ClickEvent, the counter for the click event is incremented. Whereas, in case of the HoverEvent, its respective counter is incremented. Otherwise, you should look out for a warning. You can also make type decisions, using value.(typeName) to convert the empty interface to the underlying type. This is going to panic if you get the type wrong. The other way and the safer one is to use the comma,ok idiom. The comma,ok idiom works like an if-else statement. If the passed key is found in the map, it returns the value; otherwise, it returns zero.

Listing 5-9. Go Recipe for Using the Marshal Function

```go
package main

import (
        "fmt"
        "log"
)

type ClickEvent struct {
        // ...
}
```

```go
type HoverEvent struct {
        // ...
}

var eventCounts = make(map[string]int) //type->count

func recordEvent(evt interface{}) {
        switch evt.(type) {
        case *ClickEvent:
                eventCounts["click"]++
        case *HoverEvent:
                eventCounts["hover"]++
        default:
                log.Printf("warning: unknown event: %#v of type
                %T\n", evt, evt)
        }
}

func main() {
        recordEvent(&ClickEvent{})
        recordEvent(&HoverEvent{})
        recordEvent(&ClickEvent{})
        recordEvent(3)

        fmt.Println("event counts", eventCounts)
}

/*Output:

2022/02/15 00:08:22 warning: unknown event: 3 of type int
event counts map[click:2 hover:1]
*/
```

Generics

Generics, which is code that is independent of the specific types being used, were added to the Go version 1.18. Generics allow functions or types to be able to take up several types defined in their generic form.

Suppose you want to write your own logging system. As shown in Listing 5-10, you first define the possible log levels in the system—debug, warning, and error—using the LogLevel type. In other languages, you might use enum; however, in Go, you use IOTA. IOTA is an identifier used with constants to simplify constant definitions that use auto-increment. The IOTA keyword represents an integer constant starting from zero. In the following code, you define a user type LogLevel as an unsigned integer of eight bits, i.e., uint8.

Using the const clause, you can define the three desired levels—DebugLevel, WarningLevel, and ErrorLevel. Here, because of iota, you want to start at zero, so DebugLevel is going to be one. The other values in the same const clause get an increasing value of iota. So the WarningLevel is iota+two and the ErrorLevel will be iota+3. You also want a nice string representation. For this, the String() function is going to implement the fmt.Stringer interface. The String() function returns a string. Here, a switch statement checks the log level. Note that the example uses %d and not %s, because doing so will result in an infinite recursion.

Listing 5-10. Go Recipe for Using Generics in Go

```
package main

import "fmt"

//LogLevel is a logging level
type LogLevel uint8
```

```go
//possible log levels
const (
        DebugLevel LogLevel = iota + 1
        WarningLevel
        ErrorLevel
)

//string implements the fmt.Stringer interface
func (l LogLevel) String() string {
        switch l {
        case DebugLevel:
                return "debug"
        case WarningLevel:
                return "warning"
        case ErrorLevel:
                return "error"
        }
        return fmt.Sprintf("unknown log level: %d", l)
}

func main() {
        fmt.Println(WarningLevel)

        lvl := LogLevel(19)
        fmt.Println(lvl)
}
```

   /*Output:

```
warning
unknown log level: 19
*/
```

Hands-on Challenge

Implement a painting program that supports the following features:

- A circle with location (X, Y), a color, and a radius

- A rectangle with location (X, Y), width, height, and color

Each type should implement a draw method, `Draw(d Device)`, that works on a device and also implement an `ImageCanvas`. It's a struct that holds the slice of the drawable items and has a draw method, `Draw(w io.Writer)`, that writes a PNG to w, using the `image/png` package.

Solution

Listing 5-11 is one solution to of this hands-on challenge. First, you define the colors `Red`, `Green`, and `Blue`. Then you declare a `Shape` struct that will be embedded in the `Circle` and `Rectangle` structs. The `Device` interface sets the pixel to a specified color.

Listing 5-11. Go Recipe Showing One Solution to the Hands-on Challenge

```
package main

import (
        "fmt"
        "image"
        "image/color"
        "image/png"
        "io"
        "log"
```

```go
        "math"
        "os"
)

var (
        Red   = color.RGBA{0xFF, 0, 0, 0xFF}
        Green = color.RGBA{0, 0xFF, 0, 0xFF}
        Blue  = color.RGBA{0, 0, 0xFF, 0xFF}
)

type Shape struct {
        //contains features that are common to all the
        drawable items
        X     int
        Y     int
        Color color.Color
}

type Circle struct {
        Shape
        Radius int
}

func NewCircle(x, y, r int, c color.Color) *Circle {
        cr := Circle{
                Shape:  Shape{x, y, c},
                Radius: r,
        }
        return &cr
}

func (c *Circle) Draw(d Device) {
        //calcualte bounding rectangle
        minX, minY := c.X-c.Radius, c.Y-c.Radius
```

```go
        maxX, maxY := c.X+c.Radius, c.Y+c.Radius
        //draw over the pixels within the bounding rectangle
        for x := minX; x <= maxX; x++ {
                for y := minY; y <= maxY; y++ {
                        dx, dy := x-c.X, y-c.Y
                        //check if the point in within the
                        circle or not
                        if int(math.Sqrt(float64(dx*dx+dy*dy)))
                        <= c.Radius {
                                //set pixel to the color
                                d.Set(x, y, c.Color)
                        }
                }
        }
}

type Rectangle struct {
        Shape
        Height int
        Width  int
}

func NewRectangle(x, y, h, w int, c color.Color) *Rectangle {
        r := Rectangle{
                Shape:  Shape{x, y, c},
                Height: h,
                Width:  w,
        }
        return &r
}

func (r *Rectangle) Draw(d Device) {
        minX, minY := r.X-r.Width/2, r.Y-r.Height/2
        maxX, maxY := r.X+r.Width/2, r.Y+r.Height/2
```

155

```go
        for x := minX; x <= maxX; x++ {
                for y := minY; y <= maxY; y++ {
                        d.Set(x, y, r.Color)
                }
        }
}

type Device interface {
        Set(int, int, color.Color)
}

type ImageCanvas struct {
        width   int
        height int
        shapes []Drawer
}

func NewImageCanvas(width, height int) (*ImageCanvas, error) {
        if width <= 0 || height <= 0 {
                return nil, fmt.Errorf("negative size:
                width=%d, height=%d", width, height)
        }

        c := ImageCanvas{
                width:  width,
                height: height,
        }
        return &c, nil
}

type Drawer interface {
        Draw(d Device)
}
```

```go
func (ic *ImageCanvas) Add(d Drawer) {
        ic.shapes = append(ic.shapes, d)
}

func (ic *ImageCanvas) Draw(w io.Writer) error {
        img := image.NewRGBA(image.Rect(0, 0, ic.width,
        ic.height))
        for _, s := range ic.shapes {
                s.Draw(img)
        }
        return png.Encode(w, img)
}

func main() {
        ic, err := NewImageCanvas(200, 200)
        if err != nil {
                log.Fatal(err)
        }

        ic.Add(NewCircle(100, 100, 80, Green))
        ic.Add(NewCircle(60, 80, 10, Blue))
        ic.Add(NewCircle(140, 60, 10, Blue))
        ic.Add(NewRectangle(100, 130, 80, 10, Red))

        f, err := os.Create("face.png")
        if err != nil {
                log.Fatal(err)
        }
        defer f.Close()
        if err := ic.Draw(f); err != nil {
                log.Fatal(err)
        }
}
```

Output:

Summary

This chapter included Go recipes to give users hands-on experience handling structures and using methods and interfaces. It further covered advance topics like empty interfaces and how to deal with the IOTA type in Go.

The next chapter provides Go recipes for handling JSON formatted data that is exchanged between web applications.

CHAPTER 6

Working with JSON

JSON is one of the most popular data formats used to transmit data over web applications. Like many modern languages, Go also supports the conversion of data to and from JSON. In this chapter, we walk you through recipes for working with data encoded as JSON, especially how to encode and decode JSON-formatted data for use in Go applications.

JSON Package

JavaScript Object Notation (JSON) is one of the most popular data serialization and interchange formats. The built-in package in Go that supports JSON encoding and decoding is called encoding/JSON. Using the encoding/JSON package, you can work with JSON in two ways. You can encode and decode data using the Unmarshal() and Marshal() methods. Both of these methods work on byte slices. An io.Reader object is required for the decoder to work, whereas the encoder requires io.Writer. In Go, encoding is referred to as *marshalling* and decoding is referred to as *unmarshalling*. Furthermore, using Unmarshal(), you can convert []byte into JSON format, whereas Marshal() converts JSON-formatted data into []byte. The conversion between the different Go types and JSON is defined by the encoding/json package, as shown in Table 6-1.

Table 6-1. *Conversion Between the Different Go Types and JSON as Defined by the encoding/json Package*

Go Type	JSON Type
bool	Boolean
int, float32, float64, …	number
string	string
nil	null
[]interface{}	array
Map[string]interface{}	object
time.Time	string
[]byte	string (base64 encoded)

Unmarshalling JSON with GO

To learn how to unmarshal JSON data in the Go language, you'll look at an example. Say you would like to process readings received from a weather measurement station. The readings are in the form of JSON messages containing information in the following format about time, station name, temperature, and rain:

```
{
  "time": "2022-02-15T00:00:00Z",
  "station": "DS9",
  "temperature": 21.6,
  "rain": 0
}
```

You can use Listing 6-1 to achieve this goal. The first step is to define a struct named Record that has the Time, Station, Temperature, and Rain member fields. This struct will be used to store the readings received from a weather station. Note that the name the member fields of the struct are capitalized. This is because we intend to export them, i.e., make them accessible to other parts of the program. In Go, the json package contains the heuristics for conversion of JSON-formatted data from uppercase to lowercase, so you don't have to worry about this. The readRecord() function reads and decodes the JSON data from the received readings. It takes an io.Reader object as input and returns a struct instance of the Record type along with any error if one occurs. Within the readRecord() function, an empty record is created. Furthermore, as with the io.reader object, we used the decoder to decode the JSON data received. The decoder will decode as well as store the result in the struct instance called rec, passing it as a pointer with any errors.

Listing 6-1. Go Recipe for Using a JSON Package

```go
package main

import (
        "encoding/json"
        "fmt"
        "io"
        "log"
        "os"
        "time"
)

//Record is a weather record
type Record struct {
        Time    time.Time
        Station string
        Temperature    float64 //`json: "temperature"` //celsius
        Rain    float64 //millimeter
}
```

```go
func readRecord(r io.Reader) (Record, error) {
        var rec Record
        dec := json.NewDecoder(r)
        if err := dec.Decode(&rec); err != nil {
                return Record{}, err
        }
        return rec, nil
}

func main() {
        file, err := os.Open("record.json")
        fmt.Printf("file: %v\n", file)
        if err != nil {
                log.Fatal(err)
        }
        defer file.Close()

        rec, err := readRecord(file)
        if err != nil {
                log.Fatal(err)
        }

        fmt.Printf("%+v\n", rec)
}

/*Output:

{Time:2022-02-02 00:00:00 +0000 UTC Station: DS9
Temp:21.6 Rain:0}
*/
```

Parsing Complex JSON with Go

In some cases, the JSON response can be too complex. Say you have an API that gets the status of a list of stations. The JSON response is shown here:

```
{
    "lastCheckTime": "2022-02-15 09:20:15 PM",
    "stations":[
        {
            "id":3,
            "name": "station 3",
            "status": "Active",
            "statusKey": 1,
            "lastCheck": {
                "time": "2016-01-22 04:30:15 PM",
                "success": true
            }
        },
        {
            "id":1,
            "name": "station 2",
            "status": "Active",
            "lastCheck": {
                "time": "2020-01-22 04:32:41 PM",
                "success": true
            }
        },
    ]
}
```

From this JSON response, say you want to print the names of all the stations whose last check is more than a certain time. To achieve this goal, use Listing 6-2. In the laggingStations() function, instead of writing a

163

specific type for each message in the JSON, you use an anonymous struct called reply. This structure contains the lastCheckTime as well as the station detail. Be careful to ensure that the name of the fields in the struct match the names in the JSON. Then you have stations, which is a slice of struct that has a name, status, and lastCheckTime, which is again a struct with a member field called time of string type. This example uses time as a string because the time format in the JSON message does not match how Go encodes times in JSON.

Listing 6-2. Go Recipe for Parsing Complex JSON in Go

```go
package main

import (
        "encoding/json"
        "fmt"
        "io"
        "log"
        "os"
        "time"
)

/*{
        "lastCheckTime": "2022-02-15 09:20:15 PM",
        "stations":[
                {
                        "id":3,
                        "name": "station 3",
                        "status": "Active",
                        "statusKey": 1,
                        "lastCheck": {
```

```
                                "time": "2016-01-22 04:30:15 PM",
                                "success": true

                        }
                },
                {

                        "id":1,
                        "name": "station 2",
                        "status": "Active",
                        "lastCheck": {
                                "time": "2020-01-22 04:32:41 PM",
                                "success": true

                        }
                },

        ]

}
*/
//laggingStations return stations that are lagging in their
check time
func laggingStations(r io.Reader, timeout time.Duration)
([]string, error) {
        var reply struct {
                LastCheckTime string
                Stations      []struct {
                        Name      string
                        Status    string
                        LastCheck struct {
                                Time string
                        }
                }
        }
```

```go
        dec := json.NewDecoder(r)
        if err := dec.Decode(&reply); err != nil {
                return nil, err
        }

        checkTime, err := parseTime(reply.LastCheckTime)
        if err != nil {
                return nil, err
        }

        var lagging []string
        for _, station := range reply.Stations {
                if station.Status != "Active" {
                        continue
                }
                lastCheck, err := parseTime(station.
                LastCheck.Time)
                if err != nil {
                        return nil, err
                }
                if checkTime.Sub(lastCheck) > timeout {
                        lagging = append(lagging, station.Name)
                }
        }
        return lagging, nil
}

func parseTime(ts string) (time.Time, error) {
        return time.Parse("2006-01-02 15:04:05 PM", ts)
}

func main() {
        file, err := os.Open("stations.json")
        if err != nil {
```

```
            log.Fatal(err)
    }
    defer file.Close()

    lagging, err := laggingStations(file, time.Minute)
    if err != nil {
            log.Fatal(err)
    }

    for _, name := range lagging {
            fmt.Println(name)
    }
}
```

/*Output:

```
station 3
*/
```

Marshalling JSON with Go

Not all Go types can be converted to JSON, and in some cases you'll need
a different JSON coding for your types. If you like custom serialization
for your types, you need to implement the json.Marshaler interface. If
you also like to support unmarshalling, you need to implement json.
Unmarshaler. Listing 6-3 shows how to achieve this. Say you have
Quantity, which is a struct with the value and unit member fields. You
want to encode it as a string such as 42.192km, instead of as JSON objects
with two fields. For this, you define the MarshalJSON() function on the
Quantity type. It returns a byte slice and a possible error. This function
has three steps. First, you validate that the value is not an empty unit.
Second, you convert the type to a type that is recognized by JSON. In this
case, we use %f to convert the struct into a string. The last step, we use
the built-in json.Marshal() to convert the string to JSON.

Listing 6-3. Go Recipe for Marshalling JSON in Go

```go
package main

import (
        "encoding/json"
        "fmt"
        "os"
)

//Quantity is combination of value and unit (e.g. 2.7cm)
type Quantity struct {
        Value float64
        Unit  string
}

//MarshalJSON implements the json.Marshaler interface
//Example encoding: "42.192km"
func (q *Quantity) MarshalJSON() ([]byte, error) {
        if q.Unit == "" {
                return nil, fmt.Errorf("empty unit")
        }
        text := fmt.Sprintf("%f%s", q.Value, q.Unit)
        return json.Marshal(text)
}

func main() {
        q := Quantity{1.78, " meter"}
        json.NewEncoder(os.Stdout).Encode(&q) //"1.780000meter"
}

    /*Output:

1.780000meter
*/
```

Handling Missing Values and Zeros in JSON

The encoding/json package will only fill struct fields that are found in the JSON object. By default, Go initializes all the struct fields to their zero value. In other words, numbers are set to zero and strings are treated as empty strings. Slices, maps, and channels are set to nil, and bools are set to false.

Say you have a lineItem from a receipt, as shown in Figure 6-1, containing the price, the discount, and the quantity. You want the following logic:

- If you don't have the quantity in the JSON object, the quantity should be one.

- Otherwise, if there is a quantity, it should be more than zero.

Figure 6-1. Sample receipt

One option is to make the quantity a pointer to an integer (Quantity *int). In this case, if the quantity is nil, you know that there is no value in the JSON object. Otherwise, there is some value, but working with pointers is cumbersome and error prone.

A better approach is shown in Listing 6-4, where you define a NewLineItem() function that returns a lineItem already populated with the quantity equal to one. Then, when you unmarshal a lineItem from a byte slice, []byte, you create NewLineItem, meaning the quantity field will be one. Then you can marshal it from JSON. Meaning if there was a quantity field in JSON, it's going to override the value stored in the li; otherwise, it's going to stay one. Then you perform the value validation on the quantity field. To check the workings of this code, we pass two different values in the main() function.

Listing 6-4. Go Recipe for Handling Missing Values and Zero Entries in JSON Data

```go
package main
import (
        "encoding/json"
        "fmt"
)

//LineItem is a line in receipt
type LineItem struct {
        SKU       string
        Price     float64
        Discount  float64
        Quantity  int
}

//NewLineItem returns a new line item with default values
func NewLineItem() LineItem {
        return LineItem{
```

```go
                Quantity: 1,
        }
}

func unmarshalLineItem(data []byte) (LineItem, error) {
        li := NewLineItem()
        if err := json.Unmarshal(data, &li); err != nil {
                return LineItem{}, nil
        }

        if li.Quantity < 1 {
                return LineItem{}, fmt.Errorf("bad quantity")
        }

        return li, nil
}

func main() {
        data := []byte(`{"sku": "x3xs", "price": 1.2}`)
        li, err := unmarshalLineItem(data)
        if err != nil {
                fmt.Println("ERROR:", err)
        } else {
                fmt.Printf("%#v\n", li)
        }

        data = []byte(`{"sku": "x3xs", "price": 1.2,
        "quantity": 0}`)
        li, err = unmarshalLineItem(data)
        if err != nil {
                fmt.Println("ERROR:", err)
        } else {
                fmt.Printf("%#v\n", li)
        }
}
```

/*Output:

```
main.LineItem{SKU:"x3xs", Price:1.2, Discount:0, Quantity:1}
ERROR: bad quantity
*/
```

Using mapstructure to Handle Arbitrary JSON

Say you have an endpoint that gets job-related requests in JSON format. The request can be a start or a status request in the following format:

```
{
    "type": "start",
    "user": "joe",
    "count": 3
}
{
    "type": "status",
    "Id": "689fae62"
}
```

The built-in encoding/json package cannot handle arbitrary JSONs. To overcome this shortcoming, you can use the mapstructure external package. The mapstructure package looks just like the JSON package but instead of working on a byte slice, it works on a map from string to interface that in Go represents an arbitrary JSON object. Listing 6-5 illustrates this concept. First, you import the mapstruct package. Then you define two structs—StartJob and JobStatus. The handleStart() and handleStatus() functions handle start and status requests, respectively. The handleRequest() function takes a []byte slice as input and returns any errors. The function starts with a map from string to interface, and you use the built-in Unmarhsal() function from the encoding/json package to unmarshal the data for this map. Then, you get the value of the type using the comma,ok idiom from the map. The comma,ok idiom determines if the value exists. If the value is not there, it returns an error with the message "type is missing in JSON". Val is the empty interface; therefore, you need to convert it to a string by type assertion with the comma,ok idiom. Then you use the switch statement to determine the request type.

Listing 6-5. Go Recipe for Using mapstructure to Handle Arbitrary JSON

```
package main

import (
        "encoding/json"
        "fmt"
        "mapstructure"
)
//StartJob is a request to start a job
type StartJob struct {
        Type  string
        User  string
        Count int
}

//JobStatus is a request for job status
type JobStatus struct {
        Type string
        ID   string
}
```

```go
func handleStart(req StartJob) error {
        fmt.Printf("Start: %#v\n", req)
        return nil
}

func handleStatus(req JobStatus) error {
        fmt.Printf("Status: %#v\n", req)
        return nil
}

func handleRequest(data []byte) error {
        var m map[string]interface{}
        if err := json.Unmarshal(data, &m); err != nil {
                return err
        }

        val, ok := m["type"]
        if !ok {
                return fmt.Errorf("type 'type' missing
                from JSON")
        }

        typ, ok := val.(string)
        if !ok {
                return fmt.Errorf(" 'type' is not a string")
        }

        switch typ {
        case "start":
                var sj StartJob
                if err := mapstructure.Decode(m, &sj); err
                != nil {
                        return fmt.Errorf("bad 'start' request:
                        %w", err)
                }
```

```go
                return handleStart(sj)
        case "status":
                var js JobStatus
                if err := mapstructure.Decode(m, &js); err
                != nil {
                        return fmt.Errorf("bad 'status'
                        request: %w", err)
                }
                return handleStatus(js)
        }
        return fmt.Errorf("Unknown Request Type: %q", typ)
}

func main() {
        data := []byte(`{"type": "start", "user": "joe",
        "count": 7}`)
        if err := handleRequest(data); err != nil {
                fmt.Println("ERROR: ", err)
        }

        data = []byte(`{"type": "status", "id": "seven"}`)
        if err := handleRequest(data); err != nil {
                fmt.Println("ERROR: ", err)
        }
}

/*Output:
start: main.StartJob{Type:"start", User:"joe", Count:7}
status: main.JobStatus{Type:"status", ID:"seven"}
*/
```

175

Note that in order to run Listing 6-5 successfully, you first have to import the mapstructure package at www.github.com/mitchellh/mapstructure. In order to do so, run the commands shown in Listing 6-6 from the folder where the file containing the program shown in Listing 6-5 resides.

Listing 6-6. Command to Locally Import the mapstructure Package

```
go mod init "github.com/mitchellh/mapstructure"
```

Summary

This chapter provided Go recipes to give you hands-on experience handling JSON structured data in Go. Go provides a built-in package named json for handling data that is formatted in JSON. In this chapter, you went through recipes on using the JSON package, parsing complex JSON data, and handling missing values or zeros in JSON formatted-data. The chapter also provided a Go recipe on handling arbitrary JSON data using the mapstructure package.

Now that you know how to handle JSON data, in the next chapter, you'll run through Go recipes that teach you how to handle HTTP calls by building and authenticating HTTP servers.

CHAPTER 7

HTTP

Now that you have a good grasp of the basics of the Go programming language, it's the time to put things into action! The easiest way to do that is through web application programming interfaces (APIs). An API is a set of specifications used to communicate between two programs. APIs utilize web technologies, especially Hypertext Transfer Protocol (HTTP), to exchange information between clients and servers. Go provides extensive support for HTTP. This chapter includes Go recipes for working with the net/http package, which contains implementations of the HTTP client and server.

Go and HTTP Calls

This section looks into how to perform HTTP calls in Go through an example. Say you want to post some metrics of an application to the server containing a timestamp, CPU load, and memory. Before diving into Go code to achieve this goal, let's first look at what an HTTP response looks like. The easiest way to do this is to use the curl command from the command prompt followed by an URL, as illustrated in Figure 7-1.

© Rumeel Hussain and Maryam Zulfiqar 2022
R. Hussain and M. Zulfiqar, *Beginning Go Programming*,
https://doi.org/10.1007/978-1-4842-8858-0_7

```
>curl -i https://httpbin.org/ip
HTTP/1.1 200 OK
Date: Wed, 16 Feb 2022 09:18:01 GMT
Content-Type: application/json
Content-Length: 34
Connection: keep-alive
Server: gunicorn/19.9.0
Access-Control-Allow-Origin: *
Access-Control-Allow-Credentials: true

{
  "origin": "182.185.176.197"
}
```

Figure 7-1. *Structure of an HTTP response*

The HTTP response against the curl command includes information. The first line is the status line indicating which HTTP protocol the server is running, the status code, and an optional status explanation. This is followed by a list of headers, such as Date, Content-Type, and so on. The body of the response is enclosed in the curly braces {}.

The HTTP request looks the same, except for the first line. In the first line, you have the GET /path and then the protocol. For example, GET /ip HTTP/1.1 HOST:httpbin.org, followed by the headers, the empty line, and the request body. You're going to use httpbin.org to emulate the request to the server and a response.

Now that you know what an HTTP request and response looks like, let's dive into the recipe for this example of posting an application's metrics to a server.

In Listing 7-1, the postMetric() function takes a Metric type variable as input and returns any errors. In the function, you use json.Marshal() to marshal the metric into byte slices. Then you create a Context variable called ctx to set a timeout on the request. In this example, we set a timeout of three seconds and deferred the cancel() of the request. A constant stores the URL of the website that you want to generate an HTTP request for. The built-in NewRequestWithContext() function creates a new HTTP request with context. The NewRequestWithContext() function accepts the four parameters: context, method (POST in this case), URL, and request body. Note that the body should be a io.Reader. That's why you wrap the data in the bytes.NewReader() function.

On top of the data, you set the header of Content-Type to the application/JSON. The http.DefaultClient.Do() function calls the server and checks if any error is returned. Apart from the error, you also check the StatusCode of the request to make sure that its status is OK. After passing the validations, you can parse the HTTP response. The defer keyword ensures that the body of the response is closed when the function exits. You should never blindly read everything from the network, so you should define a maximum size, in this case 1MB. Then you use the io. LimitReader() on the body to make sure only the defined size is read. You define an anonymous structure called reply to store the JSON reply, which is the metric. In Go, an anonymous structure is a structure that does not have a name. They are useful for creating one-time usable structures. To decode the reply, json.NewDecoder() is used. In the end, you log the reply.

Listing 7-1. Go Recipe for Working with HTTP Calls in Go

```
package main

import (
        "bytes"
        "context"
        "encoding/json"
        "fmt"
        "io"
        "log"
        "net/http"
        "time"
)
```

```go
//Metric is an application Metric
type Metric struct {
        Time    time.Time `json:"time"`
        CPU     float64   `json:"cpu"`     //CPU load
        Memory float64    `json:"memory"` //MB
}

func postMetric(m Metric) error {
        data, err := json.Marshal(m)
        if err != nil {
                return err
        }

        ctx, cancel := context.WithTimeout(context.
        Background(), 3*time.Second)
        defer cancel()

        const url = "https://httpbin.org/post"
        req, err := http.NewRequestWithContext(ctx, "POST",
        url, bytes.NewReader(data))
        if err != nil {
                return err
        }

        req.Header.Set("Content-Type", "application/json")

        resp, err := http.DefaultClient.Do(req)
        if err != nil {
                return err
        }

        if resp.StatusCode != http.StatusOK {
                return fmt.Errorf("bad status: %d %s", resp.
                StatusCode, resp.Status)
        }
```

```
        defer resp.Body.Close()
        const maxSize = 1 << 20 //1MB
        r := io.LimitReader(resp.Body, maxSize)
        var reply struct {
                JSON Metric
        }
        if err := json.NewDecoder(r).Decode(&reply); err
        != nil {
                return err
        }

        log.Printf("GOT: %+v\n", reply.JSON)
        return nil
}

func main() {
        m := Metric{
                Time:   time.Now(),
                CPU:    0.23,
                Memory: 87.32,
        }
        if err := postMetric(m); err != nil {
                log.Fatal(err)
        }
}
```

   /*Output:

```
2022/02/16 17:14:31 GOT: {Time:2022-02-16 17:14:29.9096948
+0500 PKT CPU:0.23 Memory:87.32}
*/
```

Authentication and Writing an HTTP Server in Go

Some websites require authentication in the HTTP protocol. There are several methods for authentication, such as Basic, Bearer, Digest, and so on. There are also several formats of authentication, like Auth2, SAML, OICD, and so on. Go supports Basic authentication; for other authentication methods such as Auth0, you need to get a token and then must set the authorization HTTP header.

In the Go recipe shown in Listing 7-2, you are going to use the httpbin.org website to demonstrate Basic authentication. The authRequest() function takes the URL, user, and password as input. These parameters are then used to create a new HTTP request using the http.NewRequest() function. You pass nil for the body since this is a GET request. The SetBasicAuth() built-in function sets the basic authentication with the user and the password supplied to the function. To make a call to the server, use the http.DefaultClient.Do() function. Then you perform validations to check if the returned response has an OK status.

Listing 7-2. Go Recipe on Authentication and Writing an HTTP Server in Go

```go
package main

import (
        "fmt"
        "log"
        "net/http"
)

func authRequest(user, url, passwd string) error {
        req, err := http.NewRequest("GET", url, nil)
```

```go
        if err != nil {
                return err
        }
        req.SetBasicAuth(user, passwd)

        resp, err := http.DefaultClient.Do(req)
        if err != nil {
                return err
        }

        if resp.StatusCode != http.StatusOK {
                return fmt.Errorf("bad status: %d %s", resp.
                StatusCode, resp.Status)
        }

        return nil
}

func main() {
        user, passwd := "joe", "baz00ka"
        url := fmt.Sprintf("https://httpbin.org/basic-
        auth/%s/%s", user, passwd)

        if err := authRequest(user, url, passwd); err != nil {
                log.Fatal(err)
        }
        fmt.Println("OK")
}

    /*Output:

OK
*/
```

If you were to use the httpbin.org website to generate HTTP requests and responses, the results you'd get are illustrated in Figure 7-2.

Response body

```
{
    "authenticated": true,
    "user": "joe"
}
```

Response headers

```
access-control-allow-credentials: true
access-control-allow-origin: *
connection: keep-alive
content-length: 46
content-type: application/json
date: Wed, 16 Feb 2022 14:43:09 GMT
server: gunicorn/19.9.0
```

Figure 7-2. *HTTP response structure when using httpbin.org*

Let's look at another example, shown in Listing 7-3, this time of an HTTP server that accepts metrics. Here, a metric is a JSON object that has host time, CPU, and memory. In the Go recipe, you define a struct called `Metric` to match the definitions in the JSON object, that is, the struct has member fields called `time`, `host`, `CPU`, and `memory`. The `handleMetrics()` function handles the HTTP requests. It takes input in the `w` variable, which is of type `http.ResponseWriter`, used to send the response back to the client, and `r` of type `http.Request`. Within the function, you first check to see that the request is a `POST` request. If it's not, you issue an error. To limit the amount of data to be read, you set a maximum size, `maxSize`, in megabytes; this is 1MB in this case. You add the metric to the database and print out that the metric was added. To send the response back to the user, you set the `Header` of the response first. Now you create a response, which in this case is a map from a string to the empty interfaces with the `id` that you got from the server. You use `json.NewEncoder` to encode the response into `W`, sending it back to the client if there is an error. You cannot change the `HTTP status code`, so you just log the error.

Listing 7-3. Go Recipe on Authentication and Writing HTTP Server
That Accepts Metrics

```go
package main

import (
        "encoding/json"
        "gorilla/mux"
        "io"
        "log"
        "net/http"
        "time"
)

// DB is a database
type DataBase struct{}

// Add adds a metric to the database
func (db *DataBase) Add(m Metric) string {
        return "success"
}

type Metric struct {
        Time    time.Time `json:"time"`
        Host    string    `json:"host"`
        CPU     float64   `json:"cpu"`     //CPU load
        Memory  float64   `json:"memory"`  //MB
}

func handleMetric(w http.ResponseWriter, r *http.Request) {
        if r.Method != "POST" {
                http.Error(w, "This Method is Not Allowed",
                http.StatusMethodNotAllowed)
                return
        }
```

```go
        var db *DataBase
        defer r.Body.Close()
        var m Metric
        const maxSize = 1 << 20 //MB
        dec := json.NewDecoder(io.LimitReader(r.Body, maxSize))
        if err := dec.Decode(&m); err != nil {
                log.Printf("Error Decoding: %s", err)
                http.Error(w, err.Error(), http.StatusBadRequest)
                return
        }

        id := db.Add(m)
        log.Printf("metric: %+v (id=%s)", m, id)

        w.Header().Set("Content-Type", "application/json")
        resp := map[string]interface{}{
                "id": id,
        }

        if err := json.NewEncoder(w).Encode(resp); err != nil {
                log.Printf("error reply: %s", err)
        }
}

func main() {
        r := mux.NewRouter()
        r.HandleFunc("/metrics.json", handleMetric).
        Methods("POST")

        http.Handle("/", r)
        if err := http.ListenAndServe(":8080", nil); err != nil {
                log.Fatal(err)
        }
}
```

Output:

1. Open a terminal from the folder where your source code resides and run the file using the go run filename.go command.

2. Open another terminal and run the following command to send the metric to the server:

```
>curl -X POST -H 'Content-type:application/json' -d "{\"host\": \"srv67\", \"time\": \"2021-03-21T17:25:33.405271214+02:00\", \"cpu\": 0.17, \"memory\": 53.9}" http://localhost:8080/metric
{"id":"01"}
```

3. Upon success, you will get the following output on the first terminal running the server:

```
>go run code-7.3.go
2022/09/01 16:49:44 server ready on :8080
2022/09/01 16:49:50 metric: {Time:2021-03-21 17:25:33.405271214 +0200 +0200 Host:srv67 CPU:0.17 Memory:53.9}
(id=01)
```

REST with gorilla/mux

The built-in HTTP server included in the net/http package is great, but it's also very simple. At times it is possible that you can get by with just using the built-in HTTP server; however, adding external dependencies to a project is a bigger risk than you might think. Refer to the research paper at https:// research.swtch.com/deps, which is recommended reading on software dependency problems. It explains why dependencies are risky and why you should avoid them as much as possible. Even though the net/http package provides several functionalities to accomplish different tasks related to the HTTP protocol, in some cases, especially when you're writing complex APIs, it's nice to have routers with more features. The net/http package performs poorly when it comes to complex request routing, for example, when splitting up a request URL into single parameters. The gorilla/mux package comes in handy in this situation due to its capabilities of creating routes with named parameters, domain restrictions, and GET/POST handlers.

The gorilla/mux package contains the implementations of a request router and dispatcher that can be used to match incoming requests to their respective handlers. Here, mux is the abbreviation for HTTP request multiplexer. The mux.Router present in the gorilla/mux package has the capability of matching any incoming request(s) against a list of registered routes, then calling the respective handler function for the route based on the matching URL or any other condition(s). This section includes an example based on using mux routers.

Say you have a bookstore and the user is requesting a book. In response, the user gets information about the book with the book title, author, and ISBN. When they call it, they'll use /books/author/ISBN. In Listing 7-4, you start by defining a struct named Book that holds the information about the book. The handler function, handleGetBook(), takes in a ResponseWriter and the request. The gorilla/mux package contains the mux.Vars(r) function, which takes an object of http.Request as an input argument and returns a map containing the segments as the output. To extract the vars with mux.Vars() on the request and get the ISBN from the path, the getBook() function gets the book from the database. If the book is not present in the database, you log and return an error for the client. If the book is in the database, you can set the content-type to application/json and use json.Encoder to encode it back to the client.

Listing 7-4. Go Recipe on REST Using the gorilla/mux Package

```
package main

import (
        "encoding/json"
        "fmt"
        "log"
        "net/http"
```

```go
        "github.com/gorilla/mux"
)

//Book is information about the book
type Book struct {
        Title  string `json:"title"`
        Author string `json:"author"`
        ISBN   string `json:"isbn"`
}

// isbn -> book
var booksDB = map[string]Book{
        "0062225677": {
                Title:  "The Colour of Magic",
                Author: "Terry Pratchett",
                ISBN:   "0062225677",
        },
        "0765394855": {
                Title:  "Old Mans War",
                Author: "John Scalzi",
                ISBN:   "0765394855",
        },
}

func getBook(isbn string) (Book, error) {
        book, ok := booksDB[isbn]
        if !ok {
                return Book{}, fmt.Errorf("unknown ISBN:
                %q", isbn)
        }

        return book, nil
}
```

```go
func handleGetBook(w http.ResponseWriter, r *http.Request) {
        vars := mux.Vars(r)
        isbn := vars["isbn"]

        book, err := getBook(isbn)

        if err != nil {
                log.Printf("error - get: unknown ISBN - %q", isbn)
                http.Error(w, err.Error(), http.StatusNotFound)
                return
        }

        w.Header().Set("Content-Type", "application/json")
        if err := json.NewEncoder(w).Encode(book); err != nil {
                log.Printf("error - json: %s", err)
        }
        fmt.Println(w.Write(book))
}

func main() {
        r := mux.NewRouter()
        r.HandleFunc("/books/{isbn}", handleGetBook).
        Methods("GET")

        http.Handle("/", r)
        if err := http.ListenAndServe(":8080", nil); err != nil {
                log.Fatal(err)
        }
}
```

Output:

1. Open a terminal and enter the go run command
    with the file containing this listing. For example, if
    your filename is code-7.4.go then you would run go
    run code-7.4.go.

2. Open another terminal and run the following
    command to get the book details from the server:

```
>curl localhost:8080/books/0062225677
{"title":"The Colour of Magic","author":"Terry Pratchett","isbn":"0062225677"}
```

Note that to successfully run the code snippets, if you encounter any errors related to importing packages, open the terminal and run these commands:

- cd [the dir of your source code]

- go mod init

- go get github.com/gorilla/mux

Afterward, restart your IDE. For more information, run go help mod.

Hands-on Challenge

For this challenge, you must write key-value pairs in the memory of the HTTP database and its client. To do this, the list of supported functions include

- Get() gets the key from the memory

- Set() sets the key to the data as received from the standard input

- List() lists all the stored keys

You are required to implement code for the client and server sides.

For the client, you are supposed to use the flag package to perform command-line flag parsing. Also, use the switch statement to perform the appropriate function based on the input you received. For the server code, use the gorilla /mux package; the db variable database will be an in-memory map. Also make dbLock of type sync.RWMutex guard the database from deadlocks. You also have handler functions for Get, Set, and List key requests. To perform routing for the server code, you must create a router in main() and use http.Handle() to handle the routing.

Solution

Listings 7-5 and 7-6 show one possible solution of this hands-on challenge. Let's discuss the highlights of the code.

Listing 7-5. Server-Side Code for the Hands-On Challenge

```
package main

import (
        "encoding/json"
        "flag"
        "fmt"
        "io"
        "io/ioutil"
        "log"
        "net/http"
        "os"
        "sync"

        "github.com/gorilla/mux"
)

var (
        db      = make(map[string][]byte)
        dbLock sync.RWMutex
)
```

```
const maxSize = 1 << 20 //MB
//client side
const apiBase = "http://localhost:8080/kv"

func list() error {
        resp, err := http.Get(apiBase)
        if err != nil {
                return err
        }

        if resp.StatusCode != http.StatusOK {
                return fmt.Errorf("bad status: %d %s",
                resp.StatusCode, resp.Status)
        }

        defer resp.Body.Close()
        var keys []string
        if json.NewDecoder(resp.Body).Decode(&keys); err != nil {
                return err
        }

        for _, key := range keys {
                fmt.Println(key)
        }
        return nil
}

func set(key string) error {
        url := fmt.Sprintf("%s/%s", apiBase, key)
        resp, err := http.Post(url, "application/octet-stream",
        os.Stdin)
        if err != nil {
                return err
        }
```

```
        if resp.StatusCode != http.StatusOK {
                return fmt.Errorf("Bad Status: %d %s",
                resp.StatusCode, resp.Status)
        }

        var reply struct {
                Key  string
                Size int
        }

        defer resp.Body.Close()
        if err := json.NewDecoder(resp.Body).Decode(&reply);
        err != nil {
                return err
        }
        fmt.Printf("%s: %d bytes\n", reply.Key, reply.Size)
        return nil
}

func get(key string) error {
        url := fmt.Sprintf("%s/%s", apiBase, key)
        resp, err := http.Get(url)
        if err != nil {
                return err
        }

        if resp.StatusCode != http.StatusOK {
                return fmt.Errorf("Bad Status: %d %s",
                resp.StatusCode, resp.Status)
        }

        _, err = io.Copy(os.Stdout, resp.Body)
        return err
}
```

```go
//server side
func handleSet(w http.ResponseWriter, r *http.Request) {
        vars := mux.Vars(r)
        key := vars["key"]

        defer r.Body.Close()
        rdr := io.LimitReader(r.Body, maxSize)
        data, err := ioutil.ReadAll(rdr)
        if err != nil {
                log.Printf("read error: %s", err)
                http.Error(w, err.Error(), http.StatusBadRequest)
                return
        }

        dbLock.Lock()
        defer dbLock.Unlock()
        db[key] = data

        resp := map[string]interface{}{
                "key":  key,
                "size": len(data),
        }
        w.Header().Set("Content-Type", "application/json")
        if err := json.NewEncoder(w).Encode(resp); err != nil {
                log.Printf("error sending: %s", err)
        }
}

func handleGet(w http.ResponseWriter, r *http.Request) {
        vars := mux.Vars(r)
        key := vars["key"]

        dbLock.RLock()
        defer dbLock.RUnlock()
```

```
        data, ok := db[key]
        if !ok {
                log.Printf("error get - unknown key: %q", key)
                http.Error(w, fmt.Sprintf("%q not found", key),
                http.StatusNotFound)
                return
        }

        if _, err := w.Write(data); err != nil {
                log.Printf("error sending: %s", err)
        }
}

func handleList(w http.ResponseWriter, r *http.Request) {
        dbLock.RLock()
        defer dbLock.RUnlock()

        keys := make([]string, 0, len(db))
        for key := range db {
                keys = append(keys, key)
        }
        w.Header().Set("Content-Type", "application/json")
        if err := json.NewEncoder(w).Encode(keys); err != nil {
                log.Printf("error sending: %s", err)
        }
}

func main() {
        flag.Usage = func() {
                fmt.Fprintf(os.Stderr, "usage: kv
                get|set|list [key]")
                flag.PrintDefaults()
        }
        flag.Parse()
```

```go
if flag.NArg() == 0 {
        log.Fatalf("error: wrong  number of arguments")
}

switch flag.Arg(0) {
case "get":
        key := flag.Arg(1)
        if key == "" {
                log.Fatal("error: missing key")
        }
        if err := get(key); err != nil {
                log.Fatal(err)
        }
case "set":
        key := flag.Arg(1)
        if key == "" {
                log.Fatal("error: missing key")
        }
        if err := set(key); err != nil {
                log.Fatal(err)
        }
case "list":
        key := flag.Arg(1)
        if key == "" {
                log.Fatal("error: missing key")
        }
        if err := list(); err != nil {
                log.Fatal(err)
        }
default:
        log.Fatal("error: unknown command: %q",
        flag.Arg(0))
}
```

```
r := mux.NewRouter()
r.HandleFunc("/kv/{key}", handleSet).Methods("POST")
r.HandleFunc("/kv/{key}", handleGet).Methods("GET")
r.HandleFunc("/kv", handleList).Methods("GET")
http.Handle("/", r)

addr := ":8080"
log.Printf("Server Ready On %s", addr)
if err := http.ListenAndServe(addr, nil); err != nil {
        log.Fatal(err)
}
}
```

As shown in Listing 7-5, in the handleSet() function, you first retrieve the keys from the vars and defer the closing of the response body. Then you use LimitReader to limit how much you are going to write. Using ioutil.ReadAll(), you read until the limit. If there is an error, you log it. You look at the database using the built-in Lock() function and defer the unlocking until the function exits. The key is set using db[key] = data. The response is then stored in the resp variable. It contains the key and the size of the data that was sent. The content-type header is set to application-json.

The handleGet() function is also similar. When the Lock() function is used to lock a resource, only one goroutine can read/write at a time by acquiring the lock. Whereas, in the case of RLock(), multiple goroutines can read (not write) at a time by acquiring the lock. In this handler, the comma, ok idiom checks if the desired key is present in the database.

In the handleList() function, you first acquire the lock on the database. Then you create a slice for the names of the keys, iterate over the database, (i.e., the map), and append the keys and write them out as JSON.

Listing 7-6. Client-Side Code for the Hands-On Challenge

```go
package main

import (
        "encoding/json"
        "flag"
        "fmt"
        "io"
        "log"
        "net/http"
        "os"
)

const apiBase = "http://localhost:8080/kv"

func list() error {
        resp, err := http.Get(apiBase)
        if err != nil {
                return err
        }

        if resp.StatusCode != http.StatusOK {
                return fmt.Errorf("bad status: %d %s", resp.
                StatusCode, resp.Status)
        }

        defer resp.Body.Close()
        var keys []string
        if json.NewDecoder(resp.Body).Decode(&keys); err != nil {
                return err
        }

        for _, key := range keys {
                fmt.Println(key)
        }
```

```
        return nil
}

func set(key string) error {
        url := fmt.Sprintf("%s/%s", apiBase, key)
        resp, err := http.Post(url, "application/octet-stream",
        os.Stdin)
        if err != nil {
                return err
        }

        if resp.StatusCode != http.StatusOK {
                return fmt.Errorf("bad status: %d %s",
                resp.StatusCode, resp.Status)
        }

        var reply struct {
                Key   string
                Size int
        }

        defer resp.Body.Close()
        if err := json.NewDecoder(resp.Body).Decode(&reply);
        err != nil {
                return err
        }

        fmt.Printf("%s: %d bytes\n", reply.Key, reply.Size)
        return nil
}

func get(key string) error {
        url := fmt.Sprintf("%s/%s", apiBase, key)
        resp, err := http.Get(url)
```

```
        if err != nil {
                return err
        }

        if resp.StatusCode != http.StatusOK {
                return fmt.Errorf("bad status: %d %s", resp.
                StatusCode, resp.Status)
        }

        _, err = io.Copy(os.Stdout, resp.Body)
                return err
}

func main() {
        flag.Usage = func() {
                fmt.Fprintf(os.Stderr, "usage: kv
                get|set|list [key]")
                flag.PrintDefaults()
        }
        flag.Parse()

        if flag.NArg() == 0 {
                log.Fatalf("error: wrong number of arguments")
        }

        switch flag.Arg(0) {
        case "get":
                key := flag.Arg(1)
                if key == "" {
                        log.Fatalf("error: missing key")
                }
                if err := get(key); err != nil {
                        log.Fatal(err)
                }
```

```
case "set":
        key := flag.Arg(1)
        if key == "" {
                log.Fatalf("error: missing key")
        }
        if err := set(key); err != nil {
                log.Fatal(err)
        }
case "list":
        if err := list(); err != nil {
                log.Fatal(err)
        }
default:
        log.Fatalf("error: unknown command: %q",
        flag.Arg(0))
}
}
```

Listing 7-6 defines a constant that holds the apiBase. It also defines the list(), set(), and get() functions. The list() function reads the keys and prints them one by one. The set() function sets a value. The get() function retrieves a specific key from the database.

In main(), you create a new router and then route the functions. Here, the Get and Set functions have key as part of the vars in the path; whereas List is just /kv.

Output:

1. Open a terminal and run the server-side code by using the go run filename.go command. For example, if your filename is code-7.5-server. go, you would use command go run code-7.5- server.go.

2. Open another terminal and run the following commands. Remember to wait at least one minute after sending a request. After sending the set request and waiting for one minute, press Ctrl+C. Then send the list request to make sure your key was set, as shown in Figure 7-3.

```
>go run code-7.5-client.go set 2
exit status 0xc000013a

>go run code-7.5-client.go list
2
```

Figure 7-3. *Output for running the hands-on solution*

Summary

This chapter provided Go recipes to give you hands-on experience handling HTTP calls in Go. Go provides a built-in package called net/http for handling HTTP calls. This chapter included recipes on using the net/http package to send and receive HTTP requests and responses, authenticating and building HTTP servers, and handling REST using the gorilla/mux package.

A killer feature of the Go language that sets it apart from other languages is its built-in support for concurrency. This built-in support makes Go the best choice for programming several different types of applications. The next chapter explains how to build concurrent programs using the Go programming language.

CHAPTER 8

Concurrency

In modular programming, large programs are usually made up of several smaller sub-programs. For example, a web server handles several requests from multiple web browsers and serves them with HTML web pages simultaneously. Each request is treated like a small program. The ability to run and make progress on multiple smaller components of a larger program simultaneously is known as *concurrency*. Concurrent programming often requires the use of different constructs, like threads and locks, to perform complex tasks of synchronization and deadlock prevention.

Go offers rich support for concurrency. Go programs can contain multiple independent tasks operating simultaneously, all doing their own thing, while communicating with each other to achieve a common goal. In the Go programming language, independently-running tasks are referred to as *goroutines*. The use of goroutines makes your program more responsive. Compared to other programming languages, like Java, goroutines can be regarded as lightweight threads. This chapter includes Go recipes that cover the most powerful feature of the Go language—concurrency. It also explains the basics of goroutines, synchronizing goroutines, and safely sharing resources among goroutines.

© Rumeel Hussain and Maryam Zulfiqar 2022
R. Hussain and M. Zulfiqar, *Beginning Go Programming*,
https://doi.org/10.1007/978-1-4842-8858-0_8

Understanding Goroutines

In Go, goroutines and channels are used to achieve concurrency. A goroutine is the smallest entity that can perform execution both simultaneously and independently alongside any other goroutines that may be present in a Go program. Put in simpler words, every task that is running concurrently in Go is referred to as a *goroutine*. Channels are used to get data from goroutines in an efficient and concurrent manner. Channels also provide goroutines with a point of reference and help different goroutines communicate.

A goroutine can be considered a lightweight thread. However, the cost of creating goroutines is far less than that required for a thread. Also, every Go program contains at minimum one goroutine, known as the *main goroutine*, which is responsible for executing the program. All the goroutines initiated by a program work under the main goroutine. Hence, when the main goroutine is terminated, the goroutines present in the associated Go program are also terminated. Furthermore, goroutines always operate in the background.

Compared to other high-level programming languages that use threads for multitasking, goroutines have several advantages. Complexity and brittleness are some of the biggest drawbacks of using threads for achieving high concurrency. Moreover, threads can also lead to hidden deadlocks and race conditions, the cause of which can be almost impossible to find. Some of the major advantages of goroutines over threads are listed here:

- **Extremely cheap in terms of resources:** Goroutines require only a few kilobytes of space on the stack. Furthermore, unlike threads, where the stack size is fixed, with goroutines, the stack can grow or shrink based on the requirements of the application.

- **Fewer OS threads required for multiplexing:**
  Goroutines require a fewer number of OS threads
  for multiplexing. It is possible for only one thread to
  exist in a program with several goroutines running
  in it. If a goroutine in a thread moves into a blocking
  state, e.g., it's waiting for input from the user, a new
  OS thread is spun and the remaining goroutines are
  moved to this thread. All these details are taken care of
  by the Go runtime and abstracted by an API from the
  programmers.

- **Channels for communication:** Channels are used
  to communicate among the different goroutines.
  Channels are designed to preclude race conditions
  from when goroutines access shared memory.
  Channels can be thought of as a pipe used by
  goroutines to communicate.

Converting Sequential Code into Concurrent Code

Before you start writing concurrent code, start by writing sequential code. Sequential code is much simpler and easier to understand and maintain. Move to concurrent code only when you have a need for the extra performance.

Suppose you have a web server that returns one CSV file per day with some information about taxi rides. The CSV file contains the data shown in Figure 8-1. It contains information regarding the start of the ride, the end of the ride, the distance covered, and the number of passengers. You want to calculate the distance for a whole month, so you need to call the API per day.

```
start,end,distance,passengers
2021-02-01T00:00:03,2021-02-01T00:00:20,3.14,1
2021-02-01T00:00:06,2021-02-01T00:00:23,3.14,1
2021-02-01T00:00:09,2021-02-01T00:00:26,3.14,1
2021-02-01T00:00:12,2021-02-01T00:00:29,3.14,1
2021-02-01T00:00:15,2021-02-01T00:00:32,3.14,1
2021-02-01T00:00:18,2021-02-01T00:00:35,3.14,1
2021-02-01T00:00:21,2021-02-01T00:00:38,3.14,1
2021-02-01T00:00:24,2021-02-01T00:00:41,3.14,1
2021-02-01T00:00:27,2021-02-01T00:00:44,3.14,1
```

Figure 8-1. *Data format in the CSV file for taxi rides*

HTTP Server Code

Listing 8-1 depicts the Go recipe for the HTTP server to run this example.

Listing 8-1. HTTP Server Code

```go
package main

import (
        "encoding/csv"
        "fmt"
        "io"
        "log"
        "net/http"
        "strconv"
        "time"
)

func dayDistance(r io.Reader) (float64, error) {
        rdr := csv.NewReader(r)
        total, lNum := 0.0, 0
        for {
                //2021-01-02T23:58:36,2021-01-02T23:58:40,3.41,1
                fields, err := rdr.Read()
```

```
                if err == io.EOF {
                        break
                }

                if err != nil {
                        return 0, err
                }

                lNum++
                if lNum == 1 {
                        continue // skip header
                }

                dist, err := strconv.ParseFloat(fields[2], 64)
                if err != nil {
                        return 0, err
                }

                total += dist
        }

        return total, nil
}

func monthDistance(month time.Time) (float64, error) {
        totalDistance := 0.0
        date := month
        for date.Month() == month.Month() {
                url := fmt.Sprintf("http://localhost:8080/%s",
                date.Format("2006-01-02"))
                resp, err := http.Get(url)
                if err != nil {
                        return 0, err
                }
```

```go
            if resp.StatusCode != http.StatusOK {
                    return 0, fmt.Errorf("bad status: %d
                    %s", resp.Request.Response.StatusCode,
                    resp.Status)
            }

            defer resp.Body.Close()
            dist, err := dayDistance(resp.Body)
            if err != nil {
                    return 0, err
            }
            totalDistance += dist
            date = date.Add(24 * time.Hour)
    }

    return totalDistance, nil
}

func main() {
    month := time.Date(2021, 2, 1, 0, 0, 0, 0, time.UTC)

    start := time.Now()
    dist, err := monthDistance(month)
    if err != nil {
            log.Fatal(err)
    }
    duration := time.Since(start)
    fmt.Printf("distance=%.2f, duration=%v\n", dist,
    duration)
}
```

Sequential Code

Let's start with the sequential code, as shown in Listing 8-2.

Listing 8-2. Sequential Code Without the Use of Goroutines

```go
package main

import (
        "encoding/csv"
        "fmt"
        "io"
        "log"
        "net/http"
        "strconv"
        "time"
)

func dayDistance(r io.Reader) (float64, error) {
        rdr := csv.NewReader(r)
        total, lNum := 0.0, 0
        for {
                //2021-01-02T23:58:36,2021-01-02T23:58:40,3.41,1
                fields, err := rdr.Read()
                if err == io.EOF {
                        break
                }

                if err != nil {
                        return 0, err
                }

                lNum++
                if lNum == 1 {
                        continue // skip header
                }
```

```
                dist, err := strconv.ParseFloat(fields[2], 64)
                if err != nil {
                        return 0, err
                }

                total += dist
        }

        return total, nil
}

type result struct {
        date time.Time
        dist float64
        err  error
}

func dateWorker(date time.Time, ch chan<- result) {
        res := result{date: date}
        defer func() {
                ch <- res
        }()

        url := fmt.Sprintf("http://localhost:8080/%s",
        date.Format("2006-01-02"))
        resp, err := http.Get(url)
        if err != nil {
                res.err = err
                return
        }

        if resp.StatusCode != http.StatusOK {
                res.err = fmt.Errorf("bad status: %d %s",
                resp.Request.Response.StatusCode, resp.Status)
```

```
                return
        }

        defer resp.Body.Close()
        res.dist, res.err = dayDistance(resp.Body)
}

func monthDistance(month time.Time) (float64, error) {
        numWorkers, ch := 0, make(chan result)
        date := month
        for date.Month() == month.Month() {
                go dateWorker(date, ch)
                numWorkers++
                date = date.Add(24 * time.Hour)
        }

        totalDistance := 0.0
        for i := 0; i < numWorkers; i++ {
                res := <-ch
                if res.err != nil {
                        return 0, res.err
                }
                totalDistance += res.dist
        }

        return totalDistance, nil
}

func main() {
        month := time.Date(2021, 2, 1, 0, 0, 0, 0, time.UTC)

        start := time.Now()
        dist, err := monthDistance(month)
        if err != nil {
```

```
            log.Fatal(err)
    }
    duration := time.Since(start)
    fmt.Printf("distance=%.2f, duration=%v\n", dist,
    duration)
}
```

Output:

```
distance=2532096.00, duration=1.7266259s
```

In Listing 8-2, the monthDistance() function calculates and returns the total distance covered in the month specified as the function input parameter. Within the function, you use a for loop to iterate over the rides in the same month and construct the URL for that day. Then you use the http.Get() function to generate a request to get the data. Some error checking is also performed to check if the response received was good or not. If everything is fine, you then calculate the totalDistance and move to the next day. The for loop iterates until the end of the month.

This code shown in Listing 8-2 is pretty simple and performs in approximately two seconds. However, if two seconds is not fast enough, you can make changes to the code to make it concurrent. Let's convert this sequential code into a concurrent version, as shown in Listing 8-2. To achieve concurrency, we are going to run a goroutine per day. This is done by splitting the sequential algorithm into two parts. The first part is generating the work or spinning the workers. The second part is gathering the results.

Listing 8-3. Concurrent Code Using Goroutines

```
package main

import (
        "fmt"
        "log"
```

```go
        "net/http"
        "time"
)

const timeFmt = "2006-01-02T15:04:05"

func handler(w http.ResponseWriter, r *http.Request) {
        s := r.URL.Path[1:] // trim leading /

        day, err := time.Parse("2006-01-02", s)
        if err != nil {
                msg := fmt.Sprintf("bad date: %q", s)
                log.Printf("error: %s", msg)
                http.Error(w, msg, http.StatusBadRequest)
                return
        }

        fmt.Fprintf(w, "start,end,distance,passengers\n")

        start := day
        nextDay := day.Add(24 * time.Hour)
        for start.Before(nextDay) {
                start = start.Add(3 * time.Second)
                end := start.Add(17 * time.Second)
                distance := 3.14
                passengers := 1
                fmt.Fprintf(w, "%s,%s,%.2f,%d\n", start.
                Format(timeFmt), end.Format(timeFmt), distance,
                passengers)
        }
}

func main() {
    http.HandleFunc("/", handler)
```

```
    if err := http.ListenAndServe(":8080", nil); err != nil {
        log.Fatal(err)
    }
}
```

Output:

```
distance=2532096.00, duration=1.0311312s
```

Within monthDistance(), the first statement is used to spin the workers. You specify the number of workers to be created and a channel to get the results. The keyword chan is used to create channels. For every date, you spin a worker, increment the number of workers, and then move forward to the next date. The dateWorker() function will return a result indicating happened. Since you get the results back in an unspecified order, you need to return as much information as you can in the result. So Unlike the previous sequential code, now you return the date, the distance, and any errors, using the resulting struct.

The result{date: date} statement initializes a result with the date. The defer function will send the result back to a channel. Note that channels are type conduits through which you can send and receive values with the channel operator, <-. Then, you create the URL, check for errors, and finally, add the date and the error to the result.

Back to the second part of the concurrent algorithm, in monthDistance(), you gather the results. First, you initialize the total distance to zero and run the number of walkers. You then read the results from the channel using the channel operator (<-). If there are any errors, you return the error or update the distance. Finally, in the end, you return the totalDistance.

Upon running this concurrent code, you will notice that there was a significant drop in the running time; for example, from 1.7 seconds to 1. This is an overall improvement of 58.8 percent in performance. Note that the running time will be different from machine to machine.

Using Goroutines with Shared Resources

Even though goroutines allow you to perform concurrent operations easily, you have to be very careful when using goroutines that access shared resources, like variables. For example, it is possible for two different goroutines to concurrently access the same variable, where one might be adding something to the value of the variable and the other one subtracting from it. It is important to make sure that when one goroutine is making changes to the variable, the other one cannot access the variable until the first goroutine has finished changing the variable. This section covers the various problems that arise when multiple goroutines try to simultaneously access a shared resource. It also covers the different techniques used to resolve these issues.

Seeing the Impact of Shared Resources on Goroutines

To see the impact of shared resources on goroutines, consider the program shown in Listing 8-4. In this example program, there is a global variable called balanceAmount and two functions called creditToBalance and debitFromBalance that are called simultaneously as goroutines. The creditToBalance function adds 1000 to the balanceAmount, whereas debitFromBalance subtracts 1000 from it.

Listing 8-4. Go Recipe Illustrating the Impact of Shared Resources on Goroutines

```
package main

import (
        "fmt"
        "math/rand"
        "time"
)
```

```go
var balanceAmount int

func creditToBalance() {
        for i := 0; i < 5; i++ {
                balanceAmount += 1000
                time.Sleep(time.Duration(rand.Intn(100)) *
                        time.Millisecond)
                fmt.Println("Balance After Credit: ",
                balanceAmount)
    }
}
func debitFromBalance() {
        for i := 0; i < 5; i++ {
                balanceAmount -= 1000
                time.Sleep(time.Duration(rand.Intn(100)) *
                        time.Millisecond)
                fmt.Println("Balance After Debit: ",
                balanceAmount)
        }
}
func main() {
        balanceAmount = 3000
        fmt.Println("Initial balance: ", balanceAmount)
        go creditToBalance()
        go debitFromBalance()
        fmt.Scanln()
}
```

/*Output:

```
Initial balance:  3000
Balance After Credit:  3000
Balance After Debit:  3000
Balance After Credit:  3000
Balance After Debit:  4000
Balance After Debit:  3000
Balance After Debit:  2000
Balance After Credit:  1000
Balance After Debit:  2000
Balance After Credit:  2000
Balance After Credit:  3000
*/
```

When you run Listing 8-4, you'll notice that the output is not as desired and is erroneous. One of the first visible errors is in the second line of the output. Upon looking closely, you'll notice that the initial balance displayed on the first line is 3000, which is correct. However, in the second line, the balance should have been 4000, but it displays 3000, which is incorrect. This happens because in the `creditToBalance()` function, after the 1000 is added to the `balanceAmount` (i.e., updated to 4000), there is a delay for a random amount of time before the updated value of `balanceAmount` is displayed on the console. This delay is caused due to the following statement:

```
time.Sleep(time.Duration(rand.Intn(100))*time.Millisecond)
```

The `debitFromBalance()` function used this delay to subtract 1000 from `balanceAmount`, updating its value to 3000. When the `creditToBalance()` resumes its task to print the value stored in `balanceAmount`, instead of 4000, it displays 3000. Even though the final value printed for `balanceAmount` is 3000, this program can still not be considered safe, because the values printed during the execution process are incorrect. Also, because of the access to the same resource, the balanceAmount variable goes into an inconsistent state.

Accessing Shared Resources Using Mutual Exclusion

As mentioned, whenever more than one goroutine is simultaneously accessing the same shared resource, it is critical to ensure that only one goroutine can access the resource at a time. To avoid the resource from going into an inconsistent state and race conditions, the concept of mutual exclusion (also called *mutex*) comes into action.

Go supports mutual exclusion by providing the mutex type in the sync package. In Go, mutex provides the locking mechanism required to make sure that race conditions do not occur. It ensures that, at any point in time, only one goroutine is running in the critical section of code. By critical section, we mean any part of the code where two or more goroutines cannot execute simultaneously. When the mutual exclusion lock is gained by one goroutine, the other goroutines have to wait until the lock is released to access the shared resource. Let's make changes to the program from the previous section to illustrate the concept of mutual exclusion through the use of the mutex type.

Listing 8-5 illustrates how a mutex object can be used to enclose the critical section of the code. This ensures that when one goroutine is executing a block of code, no other block can be executed.

Listing 8-5. Go Recipe for Accessing Shared Resources Using Mutual Exclusion

```go
package main

import (
        "fmt"
        "math/rand"
        "sync"
        "time"
)

var balanceAmount int
var mutex = &sync.Mutex{}

func creditToBalance() {
        for i := 0; i < 5; i++ {
                mutex.Lock()
                balanceAmount += 1000
                time.Sleep(time.Duration(rand.Intn(100)) *
                time.Millisecond)
                fmt.Println("Balance After Credit: ",
                balanceAmount)
                mutex.Unlock()
        }
}
func debitFromBalance() {
        for i := 0; i < 5; i++ {
                mutex.Lock()
                balanceAmount -= 1000
                time.Sleep(time.Duration(rand.Intn(100)) *
                time.Millisecond)
                fmt.Println("Balance After Debit: ",
                balanceAmount)
```

```
                mutex.Unlock()
        }
}
func main() {
        balanceAmount = 3000
        fmt.Println("Initial balance: ", balanceAmount)
        go creditToBalance()
        go debitFromBalance()
        fmt.Scanln()
}
```

   /*Output:

```
Initial balance:  3000
Balance After Credit:  4000
Balance After Credit:  5000
Balance After Debit:  4000
Balance After Debit:  3000
Balance After Credit:  4000
Balance After Credit:  5000
Balance After Debit:  4000
Balance After Debit:  3000
Balance After Credit:  4000
Balance After Debit:  3000
*/
```

In this code, Lock() and Unlock() are built-in functions that can be used with a mutex type object and can mark the start and end of a critical section of the program. When one goroutine acquires a mutex lock, all the other goroutines are barred from executing any code that is protected by that mutex. They are hence forced into waiting until the lock is released. Therefore, the output of this program is as you'd expect.

Modifying Shared Resources Using Atomic Counters

Other than using the mutex type to mark critical sections of a program, Go also provides mechanisms through which you can perform changes to shared variables but in a thread-safe manner. These are called *atomic counters*. Atomic counters are routines that allow you to perform mathematical operations on variables one thread at a time. Go provides the sync/atomic package, which contains different low-level atomic memory primitives that can be handy when implementing synchronization algorithms. However, great caution is required to ensure that these functions are used correctly. Other than certain particular low-level applications, it is always recommended to write synchronization algorithms using channels or functionalities provided by the sync package.

Let's look at an example to learn how to use the atomic package in Go programs. Let's say you host a web server that is used by multiple people to upload files. Suppose you want to keep track of the amount of data that has been uploaded to the server. In order to accomplish this task, the sync/atomic package can be used. The sync/atomic contains different low-level primitives that are faster in performance and usage when compared to sync.Mutex.

As shown in Listing 8-6, this program starts by declaring the variable totalSize of uint64 type. This is used to store the total uploaded size. Note that, when working with the sync/Atomic package, you have to be very specific about sizes. Generic types cannot be used, in this case int or uint. Inside the uploadHandler() handler function, you defer the closing of the body of the response object, then read the data, then signal any errors. To update totalSize, atomic.AddUint64() is called. It takes the pointer to totalSize as input and converts the length of the data to uint64. No locking is required during this conversion, as it's very fast and done automatically by sync/Atomic. In main(), you set up the handler function and use `http.ListenAndServe()` to start an HTTP server with a given address and handler. If you're going to expose metrics, consider using the expvar package. It not only lets you automatically increment counters, but also exposes them to the web.

Listing 8-6. Go Recipe for Modifying Shared Resources Using Atomic Counters

```go
package main

import (
        "fmt"
        "io/ioutil"
        "log"
        "net/http"
        "sync/atomic"
)

var totalSize uint64

func uploadHandler(w http.ResponseWriter, r *http.Request) {
        defer r.Body.Close()
        data, err := ioutil.ReadAll(r.Body)
        if err != nil {
                http.Error(w, err.Error(), http.StatusBadRequest)
                return
        }
        size := atomic.AddUint64(&totalSize, uint64(len(data)))

        //TODO: work with data
        fmt.Fprintf(w, "size=%d\n", size)
}

func main() {
        http.HandleFunc("/upload", uploadHandler)
```

```
    if err := http.ListenAndServe(":8080", nil); err != nil {
        log.Fatal(err)
    }
}
```

Synchronizing Goroutines

When multiple goroutines are running simultaneously, it is important to synchronize the goroutines to ensure the way a program's execution is coordinated. For example, there can be two goroutines in a program responsible for getting data from different web services, and you must make sure that both of these goroutines finish their execution before the next block of code is executed. In this case, there must be some mechanism to indicate when these goroutines have finished their execution.

If you look at the following snippet from Listing 8-6, you will notice the fmt.Scanln() statement at the end of the main() function.

```
func main() {
    balanceAmount = 3000
    fmt.Println("Initial balance: ", balanceAmount)
    go creditToBalance()
    go debitFromBalance()
    fmt.Scanln()
}
```

If the fmt.Scanln() statement is removed from Listing 8-6, after calling the two goroutines, the main() function exits immediately and the balance printed is not the correct final result, as shown in Figure 8-2.

```
$go run mutex-1.go
Initial balance:  3000
```

Figure 8-2. *The effect of not adding Scanln to the end of code*

225

When multiple goroutines are running simultaneously and there is a need to know when they have completed their execution, this is called a *wait group*, as explained in the following section.

sync.WaitGroup and sync.Once

The basic synchronization primitives, for example, mutual exclusion (mutex) locks, are provided by the sync package. Note that other than Once and WaitGroup, most of the synchronization primitive types are intended to be used by low-level library routines. Higher-level synchronization is performed using communication and channels.

Defined in the sync package, the Once type object is intended to perform exactly one action. On the other hand, WaitGroup waits for a collection of goroutines to complete their execution. The built-in Add() function sets the number of goroutines to wait for. Each of the goroutines that are part of a wait group calls the Done() function to indicate that they have finished execution. While the goroutines in a wait group are running, the Wait() function can be used for blocking purposes unless all of the goroutines have finished execution. Note that WaitGroup and once should not be copied after first use.

Let's look at an example of using both types in Go programs. Suppose you have code that can update the servers to a new version of your application. Instead of updating each server one by one, you want to update all the servers concurrently and wait for all the updates to complete. Listing 8-7 depicts the updateAll() function that gets a version as a string and the hosts in a channel. Assume that you don't know in advance how many hosts need to be updated. Within the function, you start by creating a WaitGroup. Then, for every host in the channel, you increment the counter in the WaitGroup (i.e., waitgroup1), and then spin a goroutine that will decrement the counter by calling waitgroup1.Done(). Then you call the update() function to run the code to update the server. Remember, defer is called when a function exits, so the object is called first and then defer is called. The waitgroup1.Wait() function means that you are going to wait until all the goroutines defined in the WaitGroup are done.

Listing 8-7. Go Recipe for Using WaitGroup

```
func updateAll(version string, hosts <-chan string) {
    var waitgroup1 sync.WaitGroup
    for host:=range hosts{
        waitgroup1.Add(1)
        go func(host, version string){
            defer waitgroup1.Done()
            update(host, version)
        }(host, version)
    }
    waitgroup1.Wait()
}
```

A single waitGroup does not return an error; the external errGroup package can be used to overcome this limitation, if you must know the error value from the goroutine. When multiple goroutine groups are executing subtasks of a common task, the errgroup package can be very handy. It provides facilities like Context cancellation, error propagation, and synchronization.

Let's look at an example of using the errgroup package in Go programs. Suppose you host a system that lets multiple users send messages to one another. Sometimes they need to calculate the digital signature associated with a message, but this is a very rare case, as this calculation can be time-consuming, so it's required only once. Listing 8-8 shows a sample Go program that achieves this goal.

In Listing 8-8, you first define a struct named Message with three member fields—Content which is string, once which is a sync.Once type variable, and sig of string type, which will be a cached signature and will be empty initially.

227

The `Signature()` function takes a pointer to the message as input and returns the digital signature of the message when called. Since you want to perform the signature calculation only once, you call the member field of the message and then call the `Do()` built-in function to make a call to the `calcSig()` function to calculate the signature. The `m.once.Do(m.calcSig)` statement will only call the `calcSig()` function once. After that it will do nothing. This property is also known as *idempotence*. In the `calcSig()` function, the `sha1.New()` function is used to create a new hash. Then it copies the content to the variable containing the `sha1` hash and finally the `sig` field of the message to the cached signature. The "`Calculating Signature`" message is printed as output, and then the signature. When you do it the second time, you'll see only the output.

Listing 8-8. Go Recipe for Using errgroup

```
package main

import (
        "crypto/sha1"
        "fmt"
        "io"
        "log"
        "strings"
        "sync"
)

type Message struct {
        Content string

        once sync.Once
        sig  string //cached signature
}
```

```go
//Signature returns the digital signature of the message
func (m *Message) Signature() string {
        m.once.Do(m.calcSig)
        return m.sig
}

func (m *Message) calcSig() {
        log.Printf("Calculating signature")
        h := sha1.New()
        io.Copy(h, strings.NewReader(m.Content))
        m.sig = fmt.Sprintf("%x", h.Sum(nil))
}

func main() {
        m := Message{
                Content: "There is nothing more deceptive than
                an obvious fact.",
        }
        fmt.Println(m.Signature())
        fmt.Println(m.Signature())
}
```

  /*Output:

```
2022/02/21 19:59:34 Calculating signature
93c80b92baa010458540914c7324adb9e86f0eca
93c80b92baa010458540914c7324adb9e86f0eca
*/
```

Timeouts in Go

Timeouts play a very important role when your programs are connected to external resources or you need to bound the execution time. Due to channels and select statements, it is very easy to implement timeouts in Go. This section provides recipes for implementing timeouts in Go programs.

Let's say you have to write software that will be used to participate in real-time bidding (RTB). Say you have 10 milliseconds to reply to a call to the bid, whenever it may arrive. Suppose your team has written an algorithm that can find the best bid for a given URL. However, the algorithm sometimes takes too long finding the best bid. When the algorithm does not finish in time, a default bid is returned.

Listing 8-9. Go Recipe for Using Timeouts

```
package main

import (
        "context"
        "fmt"
        "log"
        "time"
)

type Bid struct {
        Price float64
        URL    string
}

var (
        defaultBid = Bid{
                Price: 0.02,
```

```
                URL:    "https://j.mp/3cbDsIY",
        }
        bidTimeout = 10 * time.Millisecond
)

func bidOn(ctx context.Context, url string) Bid {
        ch := make(chan Bid, 1)
        go func() {
                ch <- bestBid(url)
        }()

        select {
        case bid := <-ch:
                return bid
        case <-ctx.Done():
                log.Printf("bid for %q times out, returning
                default", url)
                return defaultBid
        }
}

func main() {
        ctx, cancel := context.WithTimeout(
        context.Background(), bidTimeout)
        defer cancel()
        bid := bidOn(ctx, "https://353solution.com")
        fmt.Println(bid)

        ctx, cancel = context.WithTimeout(context.Background(),
        bidTimeout)
        defer cancel()
        bid = bidOn(ctx, "https://google.com")
        fmt.Println(bid)
}
```

/*Output:

{0.35 https://j.mp/3f3Dpkb}

2022/02/22 15:46:00 bid for "https://example.com" timed out, returning default
{0.02 https://j.mp/3f3Dpkb}

*/

Note   The code of the bestbid() function is not provided, as it is out of scope of this book.

In Listing 8-9, you first declare a struct named Bid with Price and URL as member fields. You also define a default bid value to return and the default bid timeout. The bidOn() function takes as input a context object that contains the timeout for the bid and an URL of string type. The first step in the bidOn() function is the creation of a channel. In order to ensure there are no goroutine leaks, this channel is buffered. After this, a goroutine is spinned that is responsible for calling the bestBid() function. The select statement allows a goroutine to wait on several different communication operations by blocking until one of the associated cases can run. It then executes that particular case. When multiple cases are ready to run, the select statement chooses one to run randomly. This code uses the select statement to specify two cases. The first case is executed when bestBid() finishes in time and it returns the bid. Otherwise, if the context is done before you have a result, it logs the error and returns the default values.

In main(), there are two examples. You start by creating context with WithTimeout(), using context.Background() as the initial context and the default bidTimeout for timeout. The defer keyword is used with cancel()

to make sure that the context is canceled when the function exits. The first call succeeds, but the second doesn't, as the URL is not real. It times out and returns the default values.

Pooling Goroutines

There can be tasks that are CPU intensive, whereby more time is spent using the CPU instead of waiting for the network. With CPU-intensive tasks, running more goroutines than the machine cores can handle is fruitless. When resources are limited, it is best not to choose one goroutine per job and instead use a fixed pool of goroutines. This section introduces Go recipes for working with a worker pool (aka thread pool) of goroutines.

Let's look at an example to see the pool of goroutines. Suppose you want to find the median of multiple vectors. This can be achieved using a pool of goroutines. In Listing 8-10, the multiMedian() function calculates the medians of multiple vectors. In the multiMedian() function, the first step is the creation of WaitGroup. In this case, the number of jobs to be completed are the number of vectors, so you add this value to the WaitGroup. A channel is then created which will be used to send data to the workers. In order to query about the number of logical CPUs that the current process can use, the program uses the runtime.NumCPU() function. The poolWorker() is then initiated within the for loop. The data is sent to the worker pool through the channel; it waits until all of the jobs have been completed. Finally, when there is no more work to be done, the channel is closed.

The poolWorker() function takes as input a channel as slice of float32 type and a WaitGroup. By using a for loop, the poolWorker() function iterates over the values in the given channel. This for loop will terminate when the channel is closed. It calculates the median, prints it out, and then signals that this specific job is done by calling the Done() function. Once there are no more values in the channel, the program prints the "shutting down" message to indicate that the worker is shutting down.

Listing 8-10. Go Recipe for Pooling Goroutines

```go
package main

import (
        "fmt"
        "log"
        "runtime"
        "sync"
        "time"

        "github.com/montanaflynn/stats"
)

func multiMedian(vectors [][]float64) {
        var wg sync.WaitGroup
        wg.Add(len(vectors))
        ch := make(chan []float64)

        for i := 0; i < runtime.NumCPU(); i++ {
                go poolWorker(ch, &wg)
        }

        for _, vec := range vectors {
                ch <- vec
        }

        wg.Wait()
        close(ch)
}

func poolWorker(ch <-chan []float64, wg *sync.WaitGroup) {
        for values := range ch {
                m, _ := stats.Median(values)
                log.Printf("Median %v -> %f", values, m)
                wg.Done()
        }
}
```

```
        log.Printf("Shutting Down")
}

func main() {
        vectors := [][]float64{
                {1.1, 2.2, 3.3},
                {2.2, 3.3, 4.4},
                {3.3, 4.4, 5.5},
                {4.4, 5.5, 6.6},
                {5.5, 6.6, 7.7},
        }
        multiMedian(vectors)
        time.Sleep(10 * time.Millisecond) //Let workers terminate
        fmt.Println("DONE")
}
```

/*Output:

```
Median [1.1 2.2 3.3] -> 2.200000
Median [5.5 6.6 7.7] -> 6.600000
Median [2.2 3.3 4.4] -> 3.300000
Median [3.3 4.4 5.5] -> 4.400000
Median [4.4 5.5 6.6] -> 5.500000
Shutting Down
Shutting Down
Shutting Down
Shutting Down
Shutting Down
Shutting Down
Shutting Down
Shutting Down
DONE
*/
```

Hands-On Challenge

For this challenge, suppose you want to download multiple files over HTTP. However, you want to check the total amount of data that will be downloaded prior to downloading the files. You must write a function that will calculate the download size for a single file, single URL, and multiple URLs.

Solution

Listing 8-11 is one sample solution to this problem. The `downloadSize()` function will return the `Content-Length` from the HTTP header. The `downloadsSize()` function will receive multiple URLs as input and will calculate the total download size at the same time. To test this code, we used the New York City TLC Trip dataset (`https://www1.nyc.gov/site/tlc/about/tlc-trip-record-data.page`). The `gen2020url()` function calculates the URLs for the year 2020.

Within the `downloadsSize()` function, the `dlSize` variable of type `int64` is used to return the size of the downloads. An error group named g shows when the jobs are done. You iterate over the URLs and construct a new variable to avoid closure capture. Then you use the `errgroup`'s Go function to spin goroutines. Goroutines log the URL, call the `downloadSize()`, and if there are no errors, increment the download size, `dlSize`, using `sync/atomic`. Next, you wait for the error group. This is going to be blocked until all of the jobs are done. If one of them returns an error, you get an error. Finally, you convert `dlSize` from `int64` to `integer` and return `nil` for an error.

In the `main()` function, the URLs are calculated and then the `downloadsSize()` function is called. If the execution is successful and has no errors, the program will output a message indicating a download size of 2.27 gigabytes.

Listing 8-11. Go Recipe for the Hands-On Challenge

```
package main

import (
        "fmt"
        "log"
        "net/http"
        "strconv"
        "sync/atomic"

        "golang.org/x/sync/errgroup"
)

func downloadSize(url string) (int, error) {
        resp, err := http.Head(url)
        if err != nil {
                return 0, err
        }

        if resp.StatusCode != http.StatusOK {
                return 0, fmt.Errorf("Bad Status: %d %s",
                resp.StatusCode, resp.Status)
        }

        return strconv.Atoi(resp.Header.Get("Content-Length"))
}

func downloadsSize(urls []string) (int, error) {
        var dlSize int64
        var g errgroup.Group

        for _, url := range urls {
                url := url // https://golang.org/doc/
                faq#closures_and_goroutines
```

```
            g.Go(func() error {
                    log.Print(url)
                    size, err := downloadSize(url)
                    if err != nil {
                            return err
                    }
                    atomic.AddInt64(&dlSize, int64(size))
                    return nil
            })
    }
    if err := g.Wait(); err != nil {
            return 0, err
    }

    return int(dlSize), nil
}

func gen2020URLs() []string {
    var urls []string
    urlTemplate := "https://www1.nyc.gov/site/tlc/about/
    tlc-trip-record-data.page"
    for _, vendor := range []string{"yellow", "green"} {
            for month := 1; month <= 12; month++ {
                    url := fmt.Sprintf(urlTemplate,
                    vendor, month)
                    urls = append(urls, url)
            }
    }
    return urls
}
```

```go
func main() {
        urls := gen2020URLs()
        size, err := downloadsSize(urls)
        if err != nil {
                log.Fatal(err)
        }

        sizeGB := float64(size) / (1 << 30)
        fmt.Printf("size = %.2fGB\n", sizeGB)
}

/*Output:

size = 2.27GB
*/
```

Summary

This chapter provided Go recipes to give you hands-on experience building concurrent programs in Go. Go provides built-in support for concurrency through goroutines and channels. The recipes in this chapter covered converting sequential code into concurrent code through the use of goroutines. It also provided Go recipes that dig into the effects of shared resources among goroutines and explained how mutual exclusion can overcome these side-effects. It also provided a Go recipe for using atomic counters to modify shared resources among the goroutines to overcome any deadlocks or read/write discrepancies that may occur due to shared resources, as well as recipes on achieving synchronization among goroutines with the use of sync.WaitGroup and sync.Once, timeouts, and pooling goroutines.

The next chapter includes handy tricks and tips for using the Go language more efficiently and effectively.

CHAPTER 9

Tricks and Handy Tips

This chapter provides a few hacks and shortcuts that can help you get your hands around the Go programming language much more effectively and easily. These tips and tricks are related to different aspects of the Go programming language, including packages, imports, data types, and more.

Importing Packages

Other than the usual way of importing packages into your Go program, there are also some other alternative ways to achieve this goal. The following example illustrates these different ways using the `regexp` package.

- `import alias_name "package_name"` — Importing a package using this syntax will create an alias for the specified package name, in this case `regexp`. You can then use this alias to access all of the contents of the `regexp` package using the member access operator, aka the dot operator (`.`). For example, `RegularExpression`.

- `import . "package_name"` — Importing any package this way allows you to access the contents of the particular package without the need of prefixing the exported content with the package name. For example,

© Rumeel Hussain and Maryam Zulfiqar 2022
R. Hussain and M. Zulfiqar, *Beginning Go Programming*,
https://doi.org/10.1007/978-1-4842-8858-0_9

instead of typing `regexp.MatchString("m([a-z]+`
`rs", "mars"))`, you can use the `regexp.`
`MatchString("m([a-z]+)rs", "mars")))` statement.

- `import _ "package_name"` — Importing a package in this way tells the compiler to not raise any warnings related to a package being imported and unused in the code. Any initialization functions, however, will be executed. However, no other contents of the package are exported and accessible.

Check What Packages Are Being Imported by Your Application

It is a useful and practical approach to check the packages being imported by your application. However, there is no easy way of doing this. Nevertheless, `go list tool` and `templates` can be used to get your hands around this as well. Run the following command while in the root directory of your application.

```
$ go list -f '{{join .Deps "\n"}}' |
  xargs go list -f '{{if not .Standard}}{{.ImportPath}}{{end}}'
```

You can edit this template if you want the list to also contain standard packages:

```
$ go list -f '{{join .Deps "\n"}}' |  xargs go list -f '{{.
ImportPath}}'
```

Use goimports Instead of gofmt

There are two tools provided by Go that can automatically format your source code as per the Go coding standard, namely - gofmt and goimports. The former comes packaged in the standard installation of the Go compiler. The goimports tool has to be installed separately. Additionally, the goimports tool is also able to fix package imports.

Code Organization

Even though the Go programming language is comparatively easier to learn, for beginners, the standard way that Go's code is organized can be among the hardest things to understand. Clear directions about the code organization, the different places to place source code, and the different idioms that have to be followed are provided by Go. Additionally, tools like gofmt come packaged with the Go compiler, which has strict rules for not allowing successful compilation in case the code contains any unused imported packages, variables, and so on. For more information, refer to the official talk at https://talks.golang.org/2014/organizeio.slide#1 or the official docs at https://tinyurl.com/3x3hapub.

To Use or Not to Use: Custom Constructors

Custom constructors are typically not required. However, there can be times when you have to use them; for example, when setting values during initialization, you must also sort default values. To illustrate the use of custom constructors, we use an example of a logger where a default logger needs to be set, as shown in Listing 9-1.

Listing 9-1. Go Recipe for Custom Constructors

```go
package main

import (
        "log"
        "os"
)

type Jobs struct {
        Cmd string
        *log.Logger
}

func CreateJob(cmd string) *Jobs {
        return &Jobs{cmd, log.New(os.Stderr, "New Job ",
        log.Ldate)}
}

func main() {
        CreateJob("SampleRun").Print("Initiating . . .")
}

    /*Output:

New Job 2022/06/24 Initiating . . .
*/
```

Modularizing and Organizing Code into Packages

Make sure to keep in mind scalability and complexity when you decide on the folder structure for your project. In Go, every source file belongs to a certain package. Hence, every program begins with the package statement, which indicates the name of the package the source file belongs to. In the case of very small programs, the only package that's required is the `main` package. It is best practice to make sure that packages don't have long names. When a package has multiple files, a `doc.go` file should be maintained that contains package documentation. For more on best practices regarding packages, refer to `https://talks.golang.org/2014/organizeio.slide#2`.

Dependency Package Management

Unfortunately, Go does not have its own dependency package management system. This can become challenging in a Continuous Integration (CI) environment or when multiple developers are working on a project. Nevertheless, the Go community has proposed several solutions to overcome this drawback. Go Package Manager (gpm) (`https://github.com/pote/gpm`) is considered one of the simplest working solutions. It is essentially a simple bash script that can be modified are therefore copied to each of the required repositories (`https://gist.github.com/mattetti/9334318`). It uses a custom file named `Godeps` that lists the names of the packages that need to be installed to avoid dependency issues. For more information on how to manage dependencies in your code, refer to `https://go.dev/doc/modules/managing-dependencies`.

Compiler Optimizations

Developers typically use different flags, known as `gcflags`, at build time in order to know what optimizations and memory management techniques are being applied by the compiler. Listing 9-2 illustrates using compiler flags.

Listing 9-2. Basic Program Illustrating the Use of Compiler Flags

```
package main

import (
        "fmt"
)

type UserData struct {
        ID        int
        Name      string
        Location string
}

func (user *UserData) GreetUser() string {
        return fmt.Sprintf("Hello %s from %s",
                user.Name, user.Location)
}

func CreateNewUser(id int, name, location string) *UserData {
        id++
        return &UserData{id, name, location}
}

func main() {
        user := CreateNewUser(10, "Maryam", "PK")
        fmt.Println(user.GreetUser())
}
```

Suppose this file is called gcflags-eg.go. You can build this file while also passing gcflags with the build command, as shown in Figure 9-1.

```
>go build -gcflags=-m gcflags-eg.go
# command-line-arguments
.\gcflags-eg.go:13:6: can inline (*UserData).GreetUser
.\gcflags-eg.go:18:6: can inline CreateNewUser
.\gcflags-eg.go:24:23: inlining call to CreateNewUser
.\gcflags-eg.go:25:28: inlining call to (*UserData).GreetUser
.\gcflags-eg.go:25:13: inlining call to fmt.Println
.\gcflags-eg.go:13:7: leaking param content: user
.\gcflags-eg.go:14:20: ... argument does not escape
.\gcflags-eg.go:15:7: user.Name escapes to heap
.\gcflags-eg.go:15:18: user.Location escapes to heap
.\gcflags-eg.go:18:28: leaking param: name
.\gcflags-eg.go:18:34: leaking param: location
.\gcflags-eg.go:20:9: &UserData{...} escapes to heap
.\gcflags-eg.go:24:23: &UserData{...} does not escape
.\gcflags-eg.go:25:28: string(~R0) escapes to heap
.\gcflags-eg.go:25:28: ... argument does not escape
.\gcflags-eg.go:25:28: user.Name escapes to heap
.\gcflags-eg.go:25:28: user.Location escapes to heap
.\gcflags-eg.go:25:13: []interface {}{...} does not escape
<autogenerated>:1: leaking param content: .this
<autogenerated>:1: .this does not escape
```

Figure 9-1. *Sample output of compiling files with gcflags on*

One of the optimizations that can be noticed from the output shown here is *function inlining* (https://dave.cheney.net/2020/04/25/ inlining-optimisations-in-go). Function inlining is used to reduce function call overhead and is done by moving the function body to the function call. For example, the GreetUser() function is defined at line#13 and inlined at line#25. For more information about how inlining improves the performance of Go programs, refer to http://dave.cheney. net/2014/06/07/five-things-that-make-go-fast. In essence, an equivalent of the following listing is created by the compiler.

```
func main() {
    id := 12 + 1
    user := &UserData{id, "Maryam", "PK"}
    fmt.Println(user.Greetings())
}
```

Using Git's SHA to Set the Build ID

Burning build IDs into binaries is usually very useful. Using the Git command's SHA1 is one way to achieve this. The first step is to use the Git command to fetch the short version of the SHA1 of the latest commit from your repository `git rev-parse --short HEAD`. After this, as shown in the following listing, you have to set an exported variable, in this case `Build`, whose value will be set at compilation time through the `-ldflags` flag.

```
package main

import "fmt"

var Build string

func main() {
        fmt.Printf("Build ID: %s\n", Build)
}
```

Save the previous listing in a file named `buildId-eg.go`. Simply compiling the code will not set the build; you have to set the build value by using the following Go command:

```
$ go build -ldflags "-X main.Build m9163zh" buildId-eg.go
```

In order to make sure that your build ID is set, run and check your build. This build ID can then be used in the deployment compilation process of your application.

```
Build ID: m9163zh
```

The Case of Elegant Constants, aka IOTA

There are times when the names of concepts matter greatly, especially in code, as shown in Listing 9-3.

Listing 9-3. Giving Proper Names to Concepts to Distinguish Them

```
const (
    CCRamada    = "Ramada"
    CCMarriot   = "Marriot"
    CCHilton    = "Hilton"
)
```

However, at other times, you'll only need to differentiate one thing from another and the names don't matter. For example, when storing information about categories of products in a database, it is possible that instead of storing categories as string values by names, you'll want to have integer values to distinguish them because the categories of products change over time. One of the ways to do this is shown in Listing 9-4.

Listing 9-4. Using Integer Values to Distinguish Concepts

```
const (
    CatElectronics  = 0
    CatAppliances   = 1
    CatHardware     = 2
)
```

Note that in this example, we use 0, 1, and 2 as values for constants. However, these are arbitrary values and it's up to the programmers to choose whatever they desire.

Even though constants are considered important, at times they can be difficult to interpret and maintain. Due to these reasons, developers in some languages like Ruby avoid using them. However, there are certain subtle features of constants in Go that make the code maintainable and elegant when they are used well and cautiously.

Auto Increment

One handy trick to implement auto-increment in Go is using the IOTA identifier. Using IOTA essentially simplifies the constant definitions. As shown in Listing 9-5, you can use IOTA to assign the same values as assigned in the example from the previous section.

Listing 9-5. Auto-Increment Using IOTA Identifiers

```
const (
    CatElectronics  = iota    //0
    CatAppliances             //1
    CatHardware               //2
)
```

Custom Types

Custom types are commonly used in combination with auto-incrementing constants to allow programmers to lean onto the compiler, as shown in Listing 9-6.

Listing 9-6. Custom Types with IOTA

```
type Months int
const (
    January    Months = iota // 0
    February             // 1
    March                // 2
    April                // 3
    May                  // 4
    June                 // 5
    July                 // 6
)
```

As illustrated by Listing 9-7, if a Months type argument is passed to a function that is defined to take only int type as an argument, this will not work. The program will throw an error at compile-time.

Listing 9-7. Compile-Time Errors Due to Assigning Mismatch Types

```go
func Counter(k int) {
        fmt.Printf("No. Of items: %d", k)
}
func main() {
    m1 := January
    fmt.Println(Counter(m1))
}
```

Output:

⊗ cannot use m1 (variable of type Months) as int value in argument to Counter compiler(IncompatibleAssign)

The opposite of this case is also true. As shown in Listing 9-8, you cannot pass an int type argument to a function that is defined to take an argument of the Months type.

Listing 9-8. Compile-Time Errors Due to Assigning Mismatch Types

```go
type Months int
const (
        January  Months = iota // 0
        February               // 1
        March                  // 2
        April                  // 3
        May                    // 4
        June                   // 5
        July                   // 6
)
```

```go
func Counter(k Months) {
        fmt.Printf("No. Of items: %d", k)
}

func main() {
        m2 := 2
        fmt.Println(Counter2(m2))
}
```

Output

⊗ cannot use m2 (variable of type int) as Months value in argument to Counter2 compiler(IncompatibleAssign)

However, there is a twist with this situation too. When a number constant is passed as an argument, it will compile and work fine, as shown in Listing 9-9. This occurs due to the fact that, in Go, constants are loosely typed unless used in a strict context.   ,

Listing 9-9. Program to Illustrate the Loosely Typed Feature of Constants in Go

```go
func GetMonth(character Months) string {
        var str string
        switch character {
        case January:
                str = "Its January."
        case February:
                str = "Its February."
        case Tuesday:
                str = "Its March."
        }
        return str
}
```

```
func main() {
    fmt.Println(GetMonth(0))
}
```

Output:

```
Its January.
```

Skipping Values

There can be scenarios where you want to use IOTA to assign values to constants, but you don't want the values to be in a serial fashion and want to skip some values. As illustrated in Listing 9-10, you can use underscores to skip any unwanted values.

Listing 9-10. Skipping Values When Using IOTA

```
const (
    CatElectronics  = iota    //0
    CatAppliances             //1
    CatHardware               //2

    _

    _

    CatComputer               //5
)
```

Expressions

IOTA can be used for several other purposes other than auto-incrementation. One of the uses is within expressions. The result can be stored in the constant. Listing 9-11 shows an example that illustrates this functionality. In this example, << is the bitmask operator. This trick works because there is only one identifier on a single line in a const group, so the previous expression is taken and reapplied to the identifier but with an incremented value of IOTA. This process is also known as the implicit repetition of the last non-empty expression list.

Listing 9-11. Using IOTA Identifiers with Expressions

```
type AllergyMagnitude float32

const (
    PeanutAllergy = 1 << iota //00000001
    ChocolateAllerg            // 1 << 1 i.e. 00000010
    DustAllergy                // 1 << 2 i.e. 00000100
    MilkAllergy                // 1 << 3 i.e. 00001000
)
```

Tricky Constants

You might wonder what the output of defining two constants in a single line in a const group would be. For example, in Listing 9-12, what would the value of constants Value2 or Value6 be?

Listing 9-12. Incorrect Way of Declaring Multiple Constants in a Single Line in Const Group Using IOTA

```
const (
 Value1, Value2 = iota + 1, iota + 2
 Value3, Value4
 Value5, Value6
)
```

In this case, the value of IOTA is incremented on the next line instead of when it is referenced. This would mess up your code, as you would now have constants with the same values, as shown in Listing 9-13.

Listing 9-13. Output for Defining Two Constants in Single Line in a Const Group Using IOTA

```
// ValA: 1
// ValB: 2
// ValC: 2
// ValD: 3
// ValE: 3
// ValF: 4
```

Summary

This chapter provided different tips and tricks for using Go in a more effective and efficient way. These handy tips covered several topics, including importing packages, checking which packages are imported in your program, using `goimports` to format code, efficient code organization, using custom constructors, dependency package management, optimizing compilation, setting the build ID of your project via Git, and several tricks regarding IOTA identifiers.

Index

© Rumeel Hussain and Maryam Zulfiqar 2022
R. Hussain and M. Zulfiqar, *Beginning Go Programming*,
https://doi.org/10.1007/978-1-4842-8858-0

Printed in the United States
by Baker & Taylor Publisher Services